W9-BLY-461

Christian Unity
in
North America

Christian Unity
in
North America

A *Symposium*

Edited by J. Robert Nelson

THE BETHANY PRESS
St. Louis, Missouri

Foreword

Never in their history have the churches of North America given more systematic attention to questions of Christian unity than in the period since 1956. Several hundred church leaders—laymen, pastors, theologians—were then engaged in preparations for the North American Conference on Faith and Order, which met at Oberlin College in September, 1957. In attempting to explore the full implications of the conference theme, "The Nature of the Unity We Seek," these Christians of many denominations studied a great range of theological, biblical, ecclesiastical, and sociological issues. Members of the sixteen preparatory study groups in the United States and Canada wrote individual essays, the best portions of which were incorporated into final reports of the groups to the Oberlin conference, where the delegates further appropriated the most important findings in drawing up their twelve sectional reports. Furthermore, a number of religious journals solicited and published excellent articles on the conference theme, and these had their indirect effect upon the discussions and reports at Oberlin.

The present book is intended to preserve some of the most original and helpful articles which emerged from this process of study. They were not written for inclusion in this symposium, and so they do not appear in a logical sequence which develops a certain thesis about Christian unity. The reader will find among these articles a rather striking variety of viewpoints and convictions represented. Assertions made with force in one chapter are contradicted in another. Differing interpretations are made of the same biblical passages. The main arguments in one article are minimized and given only slight notice in another. And inevitably there is found a certain amount of repetition and duplication in the book as a whole.

5

I do not deplore this variety and disagreement, just because the true state of thinking and faith in the divided churches is thereby reflected. It would be sheer dishonesty to string together a dozen articles wherein few disagreements are found and exhibit them as evidence of prevailing agreement among Christians. Nevertheless, it is at times very impressive to note the agreements and similarities which do obtain in so heterogeneous a collection of writings as this.

One of the unique features of this book, I believe, is its inclusion of articles representing denominations which remain outside the organized ecumenical movement as well as those within it. Along with Presbyterian and Methodist voices are to be heard those of the Lutheran Church–Missouri Synod, the Southern Baptist Convention, and the Mennonites. Regrettably absent are articles written by Eastern Orthodox and Roman Catholic writers, not because no such articles were produced for the Oberlin conference, but because none was in quite the right form for this symposium.

Several of the chapters have already been published in periodicals and are reprinted here by permission of the publishers, to whom grateful acknowledgment is hereby made. The articles of Professor Outler and Professor Caemmerer appeared in an important series of *The Christian Century*. An 'Oberlin issue' of *Religion in Life* carried the articles of Professor Price, Dr. Kean, and Mr. Yoder. Professor Ashby's essay was in *Theology Today*, Dr. Morrison's in *The Pulpit*, and Dr. Henry's in *Eternity*. Before this book reaches the reader, Professor Taylor's article will have been published in *Interpretation*. All the rest, except for Dr. Cavert's and my own, were prepared for Oberlin study groups.

The reader is urged to study this book in relation to the Oberlin volume, *The Nature of the Unity We Seek*, edited by Paul S. Minear, and with the aid of George L. Hunt's *A Guide to Christian Unity*. These three books are offered to the churches of Canada and the United States as aids to their seeing more clearly the need for greater unity and acting more effectively to break down what still remains of the dividing walls of hostility, which Jesus Christ himself came to destroy.

J. ROBERT NELSON

6

Contents

7

Part Three
Unity to Be Seen and Experienced

Part Four
Unity in the Local Community

Part One

The Ecumenical Movement
in American Perspective

Chapter One

The Ecumenical Movement —Retrospect and Prospect

Samuel McCrea Cavert

Former General Secretary of both the Federal and the National Council of Churches of Christ; until retirement at end of 1957 an Associate General Secretary of the World Council of Churches; Presbyterian Church in the U.S.A. This address was delivered by Dr. Cavert to the Friends of the World Council of Churches, December, 1957, on the occasion of a dinner honoring him on the eve of his retirement

Forty years ago, I had my first direct contact with interchurch co-operation and Christian unity. While I was a graduate student at Harvard, aspiring to a Ph.D., William Adams Brown asked me to be his errandboy in organizing the General Wartime Commission which the Federal Council of the Churches of Christ in America was initiating. Dr. Brown was careful to explain that this was to be only a temporary interruption of my studies and that within a year I could return to the cloistered academic halls. I am still waiting for the year to end!

I. Retrospect

Forty years ago the three streams which have converged to form what we now call the ecumenical movement were all small rivulets. None of them had been flowing for as long as a decade. None of them was deep enough or wide enough to carry much ecumenical traffic. Today the three tributaries have flowed together to produce a river which, though still following a meandering course, is able to float an ecumenical ship of substantial proportions.

One of these tributaries bears the name of "Life and Work." It began to flow in a recognizable channel in 1908 when the Federal Council of Churches came into being. Here was the first official acknowledgment by a large group of churches that they had so much in common by reason of their relations to one Lord that they would come together and stay together in a common witness and in common social action in areas of agreement. Among those unfamiliar with its origins, it is sometimes assumed that the Federal Council was an organization of a wholly pragmatic and activistic interest. This is a mistaken appraisal. It represented also a rising concern for the unity of the Church. Its constitution specifically said that the time had come "more fully to manifest the essential oneness of the Christian churches of America in Jesus Christ as their divine Lord and Saviour" and declared its first objective to be "to express the fellowship and catholic unity of the Christian Church."

The outstanding contribution of the Federal Council, however, was in the field of Christian social witness and social action. This was channeled directly into the ecumenical stream in connection with the Universal Christian Conference on Life and Work held in Stockholm in 1925. The American experience in the social expression of Christianity and the dynamic leadership of Archbishop Söderblom of Sweden were the main influences in forming what came to be known as the Life and Work movement.

Although it was in the field of Christian social responsibility that the American churches found their first official expression of unity, there was an earlier movement which contributed more basically to ecumenical life. This was the missionary movement. It had planted the Church in all parts of the earth and thereby made it possible for the Church to be a world-wide community. The event which became the historical symbol of co-operation in the missionary outreach was the World Missionary Conference held in Edinburgh in 1910. It focused attention on the urgent necessity of working together in fulfilling the mission of the Church. It led, under Dr. John R. Mott's leadership, to the creation of national Christian councils in Asia, Africa, and Latin America, and in 1921, to the International Missionary Council, in which these national councils and national missionary conferences of the older churches joined in mutual aid and planning.

The third tributary of the ecumenical movement, which goes by the name of "Faith and Order," also took its rise in 1910 and was chiefly due to the vision of Bishop Charles H. Brent. Although a strong advocate of interdenominational co-operation both in the world mission and in the Christian witness in society, he felt it necessary to go further and to challenge the separation and aloofness of the denominations from one another at those points which concern the nature of the Church and its ministry.

At Edinburgh it had been agreed that the goal of carrying the Christian Gospel to the world could best be achieved by concentrating on common purposes and ignoring doctrinal and ecclesiastical differences. In the Life and Work movement, it was similarly assumed that the path of advance was for the churches to work together in practical tasks without worrying about the differences. Bishop Brent, however, felt that the differences could not thus be bypassed. The World Conference on Faith and Order at Lausanne in 1927 gave the first strong impetus to a continuing effort of the churches to understand each other at the level of their most baffling separations.

For more than twenty-five years these three streams flowed in separate channels. They were all expressions of a desire for a greater measure of unity but they had their sources in different centers of interest and pursued courses that paralleled each other. In 1937, however, a confluence of the three streams began. As a result of a consultation at Westfield College in London, under the chairmanship of William Temple, then Archbishop of York, the plan was projected which has united "Life and Work" and "Faith and Order" in the World Council of Churches. A little later, a joint committee representing the World Council, still "in process of formation," and the International Missionary Council was formed and after the World Council came into formal existence in 1948, the two bodies were officially defined as "in association" with each other. This "association" has been so real and close that a plan for fuller integration is now being considered.

Reviewing this ecumenical history, it seems to me to be almost a miracle. What has happened was so unpredictable a half century ago that we must believe that the Holy Spirit has been creatively at work in the life of the Church. The whole course of what we call the ecumenical movement has taken place within fifty years. My own generation has seen it all. The rise of the three main tributaries—the formation of the Federal Council, the Edinburgh Missionary Conference, and the resolution calling for a World Conference on Faith and Order—all occurred during my student days. It has been my blessed privilege to have known personally the original leaders of all three movements and to have observed all that has developed since.

In retrospect, we can now see what important ecumenical assets we have that our fathers did not have. First, the Christian community has become world-wide to a degree never before known. Second, that world-wide Christian community is becoming aware of a oneness that lies at a deeper level than all its differences. Third, there is the beginning of an ecumenical structure in which the oneness of the Christian community is becoming more visible to the world. As the historian Kenneth Scott Latourette points out, the World Council of Churches embraces more diverse groups in more parts of the world than any other organization which all the centuries have known. Professor Latourette also renders the judgment that in this new trend toward world-wide Christian fellowship, we have indications of "a fresh burst of life" which may prove to be fully as significant as the Reformation of the sixteenth century or the evangelical awakening of the eighteenth century.

To be at all realistic, however, we must admit that most of the great questions inherent in the ecumenical movement have still to be answered. We have become more conscious of our oneness in Christ and so have a growing unity of spirit and purpose, but we still have to discover how to give an adequate organizational expression of this new spirit.

To use a homely analogy, the ecumenical honeymoon is over. We are now at the stage of patiently developing the kind of day-by-day relationships and patterns of conduct for which life within an ecumenical household calls. But we can at least be grateful that the house in which we live has three firm foundation stones. One of them, laid by the missionary movement, is our recognition of the universal mission of the Church to proclaim the Gospel to all mankind. Another foundation stone, given form by the Life and Work movement, is our commitment to making Christ known as Lord over all the areas of our life and society. The third, laid by Faith and Order, is the emphasis on the Church as the one Body of Christ and on the resulting impulse to give a more convincing corporate manifestation of unity. None of these foundation stones, standing alone, could give a support strong enough for our ecumenical house. Each of them needs the reinforcement of the other two. All three are cemented together in the ecumenical movement that we now have.

14

II. Prospect

Turning from retrospect to prospect, I limit myself to two basic problems which seem to me to stand out as of most crucial importance.

The first problem is how to *combine concern for ecumenicity* with *concern for locality.* How are we to bridge the gap between those who see the Church in its world-wide wholeness and those who see the Church in terms of a particular place and in relation to a particular group of members? Each of these points of view is valid and essential if it is related to the other in some vital synthesis. But as of today, they tend to be "either—or." The ecumenical interest and the local interest are competing with each other. On one hand, there are ecumenists who are so deeply concerned about what is happening to the Church in general, in Europe, East Asia or behind the "Iron Curtain," that they lose contact with what the parish church in their town is doing for its own members by its worship, its pastoral work and its religious education. On the other hand, many a pastor is so absorbed in ministering to the immediate face-to-face needs of a limited number of families that he does little or nothing to lead them to a sense of world mission or social responsibility. As a result, they go on thinking of the church only in connection with the way in which it serves them and their children.

This gap between the ecumenical perspective and the local perspective appears most starkly in a church in our comfortable and complacent suburbs. It is successful by all the conventional standards. It is growing in numbers. It has a beautiful house of worship. Its preaching and its music are giving refreshment to men and women living under heavy personal strains. It is providing pastoral care to the sick and the troubled. It is helping children to grow up with at least some knowledge of the Bible. And it is easy for an ecumenical enthusiast to forget how basic all this is.

But what is this church doing to help its people understand the duty of Christians to be concerned for the world? All too often it goes on as if it had no responsibility for any of the issues of the most desperate urgency for the life of mankind. It is not stirring its members to face the racial situation with the mind of Christ. It is not making them critical of the low level of ethical integrity in our economic and industrial life. It is raising no disturbing

15

question as to what Christian citizenship means for American assistance to underdeveloped areas of Asia and Africa. It is leaving people with no vision of the Church as concerned with the character of the whole culture in which the church is set.

And how can the local church fulfill any such function unless it sees itself in relation to the world-wide church, not merely as an agency for ministering to its own members? At the present time, both the pastor and the congregation probably regard the ecumenical movement as an outside interest, an extra something that concerns only those who go to national or international conferences, "the ecumenical Rover boys," as someone has dubbed them. Many a minister would, in fact, be greatly surprised to hear that it is he who is the real representative of the ecumenical Church in this particular place. When he comes to appreciate this fact, it makes a difference in everything in that church's life—its worship, its preaching, its education of children and youth, the community as a whole, its training for Christian responsibility in the nation and the world.

How is this gap between ecumenicity and locality to be bridged? There is no easy formula, but most of the answer must be found in a deeper and more widespread understanding of the nature and mission of the Church in the world on the part of both ministers and laity. For any decisive advance in ecumenical life this seems to me to be the fundamental need.

The second problem before us has to do with *the nature of the unity we seek* in the ecumenical movement. Is it to be defined in terms of denominations working together in tasks which they recognize as common? Or is it a unity in which the separations between the denominations are to be sufficiently overcome to result in a church in which a common ministry and common sacraments are recognized and there is enough of a common structure to be visible to the world? This question implies, of course, that interdenominational efforts do not, in themselves, raise any question about the permanent validity of denominations as we see them. The ecumenical movement, however, involves an insight into the nature of the Church as, in some vital sense, a single reality given to us by Jesus Christ in and with the Gospel.

On the organizational side, this issue includes an important question about the role of a council of churches—local, state, national or international—in the ecumenical movement. Most councils have not yet seriously faced this issue. This is not surprising. The achievement of effective co-operation has obviously been the first necessary step in unity and has been difficult enough in itself without raising a debate as to whether there is a stage in unity that lies beyond co-operation.

To make the issue more concrete, let me refer to opposing views which have found recent advocacy in print. Bishop J. E. Lesslie Newbigin of the Church of South India fears that the very success of a council of churches in reducing the sharpness of conflict and securing co-operation in minor matters may make us complacent toward the divisions that remain. He warns us against the danger that programs of working together might become a substitute for unity and undercut what he regards as the true ecumenical goal. Dr. Howard W. Conn, however, pastor of Plymouth Congregational Church of Minneapolis, writing in the *Christian Herald,* comes at the matter from exactly the opposite angle. He fears that if you define the ecumenical movement in Bishop Newbigin's terms, as ultimately involving union, it "undercuts the interdenominational co-operation that today exists and is growing." Dr. Conn assumes that a united church on a national or world-wide scale, would so endanger our present freedom and diversity that churches would hesitate to co-operate if they suspected that this might lead to some kind of union.

In my own judgment, both Bishop Newbigin's and Dr. Conn's misgivings are unjustified. On the one hand, I have no doubt whatever that the progress toward unity in the last fifty years has been primarily due to the decisions of the churches to undertake various responsibilities together in certain areas of agreement, even though there were other areas in which they still disagreed. Indeed, I do not believe that we today would even be talking about unity except for our experience in co-operation. I am further convinced that an experience of enlarging co-operation is an indispensable contribution to the mutual understanding and the mutual appreciation without which no organizational form of unity will have spiritual meaning.

On the other hand, we must admit that not all kinds of co-operation are creative of unity. Much depends on the motives which impel the co-operation and the assumptions behind it. An interdenominational program which is developed merely because it will be a convenience to the denominations, or perhaps because it is too peripheral to their central interests to seem important to them, has little or no significance for real unity. A co-operative organization which operates in mutual independence of nominal member churches or comes to be regarded as a separate object of loyalty may render many good services and yet have little influence in drawing the churches together at any deep level of their life. A council of churches is creative of unity only to the degree that it is consciously recognized by the churches as their instrument in a constant quest of unity.

Until recently, most councils of churches have been content to ignore differences of faith and order and to have a wholly pragmatic conception of their function. This has been due to one of two assumptions: either that the doctrinal matters were unimportant or else that they were insoluble. This point of view was summed up at the Stockholm Conference in the statement that "doctrine divides while service unites." This conclusion, it is now clear, will not stand up under examination. As a matter of fact, doctrine does unite, provided it has to do with the great central convictions of our faith in God and his forgiving love, in Christ and his redeeming power, in the Holy Spirit and his renewing work. Actually it is only this common faith which gives any council of churches its ultimate significance. I am glad, therefore, that councils are beginning to feel that it is a part of their proper role to help the churches join in a common study of theological issues, including the perplexing differences which today keep the churches apart. In so doing, they will often be moving from co-operation in things which the churches regard as of marginal concern into the central issues of their life and thought and worship. Perhaps we have reached the point in the co-operative movement where it is not likely to go much further except as it goes deeper.

I do not mean to imply that a vast merger and an over-all union of the type commonly called organic must be the goal of the ecumenical movement, although I hope that there will be many unions within related church families. Neither do I think that more co-operation of the same kind that we see today is the end in view. We surely need a unity which goes far enough to assure a ministry and sacraments that are recognized throughout the whole Church. At the same time, we must never cease to safeguard the values of freedom and diversity. The unsolved question is what kind of structure will best secure both of these ends. The answer will not be found by making a detour around the issues of faith and order. It requires us to move straight into their midst.

My personal opinion is that at the present stage of ecumenical development we should put all our emphasis on unity rather than on formal union, but without ever allowing ourselves to become satisfied with our divided state. The unhappy fact is that we are not spiritually ready for one great Church. Before there can be meaningful union in the organizational realm, we must meet three prior conditions in the realm of the spirit:

(1) Our denominations must have a deeper mutual understanding of each other's positions—something much more difficult to achieve than tolerant good will.

(2) We must have a clearer and more general recognition of the partial nature of the truth which each historic branch of the Church possesses and, consequently, have a greater passion for the wholeness of the Church.

(3) We must be prepared to accept a wide range of differences within a united Church. Otherwise, there would always be the temptation to too much conformism, too easy a squelching of minorities, too much of the kind of unity achieved by the drill sergeant in making everybody toe the same straight line.

If I were asked to summarize in a single remark what now seems to me the main strategy of advance in the ecumenical movement, I would do so by recalling something said at Lund in 1952. It was the insistence that we face seriously the radical change that would take place in the life and work of all our churches if we were consistent with our belief that the unity we have by reason of our relation to one Lord is far more important than our differing interpretations of his will. As things now stand, we act separately as denominations in most things, and we act together in only those few things in which we can scarcely act alone. We need to reverse the process. If our oneness is the primary fact and if our divergencies are of secondary moment, then, as was said at Lund, churches should "act together in all matters except those in which deep differences of conviction compel them to act separately."

Socrates was once asked how to get to Olympus. The reply of the sage was, "By doing all your walking in that direction." His answer is equally applicable to the reaching of our ecumenical goal.

Chapter Two

Christian Unity in North America

J. Robert Nelson

Dean of the Vanderbilt University Divinity School;
former Secretary of the Commission on Faith and Order
of the World Council of Churches; Methodist Church

I.

Sectarianism is considered by many to be the hallmark of American Christianity. A visitor from abroad receives various strong impressions of the church life he sees in the United States and Canada. He is struck by the vitality of congregational activity, the vigorous support given the local church by each member, the economic prosperity of suburban churches, and the equidistance of all churches from the secular government. But it is the organized strength, cohesiveness, self-sufficiency, and public acceptance of the numerous denominations which give the Christian churches of America their distinctive character.

The historical causes for this "denominationalism run wild" are readily seen. Of primary importance is the fact that nearly all the major ecclesiastical schisms of Great Britain and the Continent were imported by immigrants. Indeed they were multiplied in America because of the persistence into our own day of various nationality groups using, albeit decreasingly, the languages of the "old country," and nursing ancient nationalistic prejudices. So the lesser movements of the lands left behind, such as Baptists and Methodists, became the major denominations of America. And the established churches, such as Roman Catholic, Anglican and Lutheran, could only hold their own as the others.

The political tenet of church-state separation and unrestrained freedom of religious expression was the second factor which made the burgeoning of denominationalism virtually inevitable. This endemic conviction, which was written into the Constitution of the United States in the First Amendment, is certainly not to be deprecated as a hindrance to Christian unity. It is most unlikely that the establishment of one or another church as the national church could have prevented the continued proliferation of denominations. But the principle of religious freedom certainly contributed to the religious pluralism of American society.

The theological emphases of the later Colonial period, which are the third cause, were so far removed from any coherent and commanding doctrine of the Church and its essential unity, and so intensely laid upon individual conversion, that there was scarcely any theological rein drawn upon galloping sectarianism. One could justly assert that the whole character of North American Christianity would have been vastly different if the renewal of the doctrine of the One Church, which is ascendant in the present time, had taken place two hundred years ago.

Finally, the rapidly expanding frontier of exploration and settlement and the general rootlessness of the pioneer population provided the conditions in which the three causes noted above could produce most fruitfully the effects of sectarian divisions.

It is quite untrue to say, then, that American Christians are inherently divisive. It is more accurate to recognize how unlikely it would have been for any Christians of whatever nationality to have preserved a greater measure of unity during the same period of time under the same circumstances.

II.

Less well known than the fragmentation of the Church in America are the many significant efforts which have been made during the past 150 years to bridge the gaps between denominations and manifest a greater measure of unity. One of the very few summaries of these efforts, and an excellent one, is given by Don H. Yoder in *A History of the Ecumenical Movement*, edited by Bishop Stephen C. Neill and the late Dr. Ruth Rouse.[1] Writing mainly about the nineteenth century, Yoder describes the increasing ardor of certain church leaders in their campaigns against denominational divisions. Alexander Campbell's energetic and prophetic ministry until his death in 1866 was more effective in arousing Protestants

---

[1]Chap. 5. Westminster Press, Philadelphia, 1954. cf. H. P. Douglass, *Church Unity Movements in the United States*, New York, 1934.

to recognize the imperative of the Gospel for Christian unity than in prompting divided parties actually to unite. His approach to unity in terms of the restoration of the primitive apostolic community, observes Yoder, was one "which was not only peculiarly American, but which has provided a continued impulse to unity into the present century." S. S. Schmucker and Philip Schaff were two towering exponents of unity who arose within the daughter churches of continental Lutheran and Reformed traditions. They were persuaded, in contrast to Campbell, that the historic doctrines and practices of the several denominations would have to be preserved and comprehended. Schmucker's widely noted appeal to American Christians was for the formation of an "Apostolic Protestant Church" along the lines we have come to know as "federal union." An eminent Episcopalian advocate of unity, W. R. Huntington, on the other hand, urged his own denomination to set its eyes upon the ultimate goal of complete union in doctrine, ministry, and sacramental practice. As a sound basis for unitive negotiations with other denominations he laid down the four principles of essential Christianity which were subsequently adopted by Anglicans everywhere as the "Chicago-Lambeth Quadrilateral": Scriptures, Creeds, Sacraments, and Historic Ministry.

The efforts of these four men were representative of numerous, widely scattered initiatives toward unity which marked the history of the churches in the nineteenth century. And they prefigured the three main approaches to the overcoming of divisions which still are to be found among the non-Roman churches of America: (a) restoration of the "simple" primitive Church; (b) comprehension of diverse traditions within a federation of churches; and (c) union and amalgamation of divided denominations on the basis of certain essential elements of the Church visible.

Of these three it is the second which has come to be known as the typically American approach. It is often maintained that Americans are activists and pragmatists, too impatient to wait for the exhaustive analysis, construction, and criticism of doctrinal propositions which are necessarily involved in the laborious intellectual struggle for the understanding and resolving of theological divisions. This generalization is largely true, but only partly so. It is true that a main current of Protestant theology in the twentieth century has had Martha rather than Mary as its proto-

22

type. It is true also that the dominant manifestation of the unitive spirit has been the council of co-operating churches in a city or state, and the Federal and later National Council of Churches in the United States at large, and that these have generally avoided entanglement in the supposedly lethal coils of disputation over doctrines, creeds, and liturgies. But these truths are usually expressed in caricature—and all caricature by definition plays up the dominating characteristic while obscuring the secondary but equally true one.

Concurrent with the dramatic development of co-operative Christianity in America has been the less clamant activity of church leaders who have believed that co-operation, being only a partial solution to the problem, requires the complementing engagement of divided Christians in the common task of seeking unity in matters of faith and church order. Those who know the story of the ecumenical movement in this century need only be reminded that the originators of the conference on Life and Work and on Faith and Order were two men whose nationalities called the caricatures of European and American Christianity into question. The chief exponent of co-operation on practical issues was the *European* Lutheran, Archbishop Nathan Söderblom, of Sweden. The patriarch of the quest for unity along the precarious path of theological inquiry was the Canadian-born, *American* Episcopalian, Bishop Charles H. Brent. And it was not a European professor of theology, but an American layman and lawyer, Robert H. Gardiner, who did more than any person in the world to bring to realization the First World Conference on Faith and Order at Lausanne in 1927.

Even though the United States and Canada have contributed their full share of leaders to the world-wide movement for unity, it is patently clear that the many denominations, with their thousands of congregations and millions of members, have been reluctant and slow to understand the challenge of the One Church against their divisions. While a few prophetic voices have been raised against disunity during the past 150 years, the overwhelming majority of church members and pastors have been wholly content to abide in their denominational isolation. Indeed, many have sought to justify such separateness on grounds of biblical evidence, theological reasoning, sociological data, and common sense.

A prominent Congregationalist, W. E. Barton, soon after participating in the Lausanne Conference, which apparently had not impressed him, declared:

> Let us recognize the unity that now exists in the Church of Christ. . . . Let us do away with our hypocritical days of prayer and confession of sin concerning disunity, and make the most of the unity that exists. . . . Jesus and John the Baptist were leaders of divergent sects within the Church. . . . We have four Gospels because no one Gospel could satisfy all divisions within the Church. . . . Let us stop wailing about our divisions and emphasize our unity.

The quotation is cited, not because it expresses a quaint and unusual way of thinking, but precisely because it is typical of the viewpoints of a great many Christians today. So far as any sincere desire for visible church unity is concerned, it would require a most optimistic mentality to assert that defensive, self-justifying denominationalism is on a sharp decline.

And yet, there *is* a moderate decline, and this is significant. Concurrent with the Faith and Order movement there has developed, gradually but insistently, a frame of mind which may be styled "denominational self-criticism." Peter Ainslie of Disciples of Christ spoke for this viewpoint at Lausanne when he said, "My denomination must grow less and less in my eyes if I am to grow more toward Christ." This does not mean that denominational traditions and teaching are to be despised and rejected of men, in order to make room for some new and unscarred form of Christianity as yet untried. It implies, rather, that the existence of so many other denominations, with their diversities of doctrine and practice, constitutes a threat to the self-sufficiency and exclusiveness of one's own denomination. And this exclusiveness, fortified by many small-group prejudices and a common but provincial ethos, militates against a full appreciation of the work of Jesus Christ in the wholeness of his Church.

This denominational self-criticism has taken a variety of forms in the thinking of American Christians. Many have felt anguish over the divisions of churches because of their impotence as an ethical force in society at large. In his brush-clearing study of America's church divisions in 1929, H. Richard Niebuhr declared, "Denominationalism thus represents the moral failure of Christianity."[2] Others have become increasingly sensitive to the liturgi-

---

[2] *The Social Sources of Denominationalism*, Holt & Co., New York, 1929, p. 25.

cal deficiencies of their own denominations and the need for the more profound and meaningful form of public worship which could be experienced in a church united. So also with the theological emphases, the moral judgments, and the separate traditions of these fragmented bodies of Christian churches—none of which can by itself show forth the wholeness and catholicity of the One Church.

III.

While it is difficult to determine the extent to which unity has become recognized in American churches as a matter of divine will and temporal urgency, it is fairly easy to discover the factors contributing to their recognition.

A. The first major influence is *the ecumenical movement* itself. Nearly fifty years after the Edinburgh Missionary Conference of 1910, when the movement is generally regarded as having begun, the imperative of Christian unity is only now commanding the obedient response of significant numbers of Christians. Many people ask whether a cause which requires fifty years to be accepted widely is a valid one. The answer is: inertia. The resistance of the churches to any radical change of attitude can be matched in few other social institutions, even when the direction of that change is advocated as essential and indispensable to the well-being and wholeness of the Church. A comparable lag of Christians behind their leading thinkers was the slow response to the world missionary movement of the nineteenth century. At first the missionary obligation, which we now take for granted, was regarded by many as an extraneous matter so far as local churches are concerned. While the sincere concern of countless Christians has not yet been directed toward the evangelistic mission of the whole Church in the world, or even of their own denomination, it can be said confidently that no church or denomination could any longer ignore its missionary responsibility with a clear conscience. Is it expecting too much that the next generation of the church will have a collective bad conscience if it fails to engage responsibly in the movement for unity?

B. The second factor to be noted is the renewed interest of American Christians in *theology*. It is now plain to most thoughtful church members that theology is not an intellectual hobby of a few professional theologians, but the indispensable and never-ending inquiry of men into the meaning of God's will. Theological work

25

is to the daily life of the Church in worship and service what pure scientific theory is to the invention and production of the wonders of this industrial-plastic-electronic era of civilization. Now the swelling stream of contemporary theological thought is characterized by an earnest effort to understand, appropriate, and interpret the Old and New Testaments. Beyond both "liberalism" and "neo-orthodoxy" is the wider, and literally more ecumenical, system of thought called "biblical theology." Because it regards the Bible as a book of God's revelation rather than man's mere experience and speculation, this theological position is inclusive of many so-called conservatives. Because it uses without fear the methods of textual and historical criticism, and is zealous to keep Christian theology in a dialogue with philosophy and the various sciences, it has also an affinity for the best in theological liberalism.

The effect of biblical theology upon the unity movement in the United States and Canada, as in other countries as well, is twofold. First, it provides a common area of conversation for spokesmen of the separate denominations, and thus has the effect of drawing them out of the ways of thought which are often stereotyped according to denominational traditions. This discovery of a common framework of discourse in terms of biblical theology has been an amazing and invigorating experience for those who have participated in ecumenical conferences or plunged into current theological literature. At the Oberlin study conference this factor was noted specifically in the report of Division I:

> The emergence of biblical theology is one of the exciting developments of our time. As we acknowledge in common the authority and constraint of the Word of God we are brought into a new measure of agreement one with another.[3]

To this renewed theology goes also the credit for having brought to modern churches a vital sense of the One Church itself. Following an extended period in which theologians and laymen of both Europe and America actually belittled the church as a historical accretion upon the pure Christianity of the New Testament, we are now enabled by biblical scholars and theologians to perceive in the Bible itself a dominant doctrine of what the Church of Jesus Christ is intended to be. And one of the essential marks of the Church, along with its holiness of life, apostolic witness, and

---

[3]*The Nature of the Unity We Seek,* edited by Paul S. Minear, Bethany Press, St. Louis, 1958, p. 168.

catholic extent to the whole range and depth of man's life, is its oneness. It is obviously not possible to find a specific biblical answer to every problem which arises today about the life and form of the churches. But as to the Bible's teaching on the necessity of exhibiting the oneness of the Church on earth there can be no valid doubt.

C. *Sociological changes* in American church life are the third influence upon the prevailing attitude toward unity. In the international conferences and studies on Christian unity it is the Americans who have been most insistent upon giving serious attention to the numerous nondoctrinal factors. Doctrine, theology, history, liturgy, ministry—all these need constantly to be examined in the light of biblical teaching and ecclesiastical practice. But the Church does not exist independent of culture; and what happens to churches in society is no less important to their movement toward unity than is their doctrinal posture.[4]

The Oberlin conference has provided the first occasion for American church workers, theologians and sociologists to deal systematically with the nondoctrinal factors in the total context of Faith and Order questions. There it was pointed out that the current social upheaval in North America, in which a young man could scarcely recognize the society of his father's youth, is contributing positively to the churches' quest for unity, even as social factors of the past have caused division. This is a fact of highest importance. The general mobility of American people, for example, has all but destroyed the idea of a settled, stable parish life. Automobiles make the parish a nongeographical concept. One family out of every four moves each year, and in its new location chooses a church without always considering denominational loyalty. In recent decades the cultural ties of immigrant groups with the churches of the "old country" and its language have nearly disappeared. The suburbanization of a great part of the population and the radical changes in rural society have likewise affected denominational churches. The great shift in the membership of social classes, because of widespread prosperity and extended college education, has had its effect. Finally, the interdenominational experiences in worship and group living of millions of young people in colleges and the armed forces have further prepared them and

---

[4]cf. address on "Institutionalism" by Walter G. Muelder in *The Nature of the Unity We Seek*, pp. 90-102.

the churches of which they become leaders to meet the challenge of the ecumenical movement. All such developments in our day help explain the growing disposition of Christians to think more about ways of manifesting the unity of the church in North America and less about defending the separate bastions of denominationalism.

IV.

It is tempting to discuss church unity in America as only a hypothetical matter. But it is wrong to yield to this overly theoretical way of thinking. Churches are not only discussing unity in general terms, but they are acting upon it in relation to other denominations in a manner and degree amazing to the uninformed person. Church unions, or mergers, have often been fulfilled in this generation, and others are being prepared. Some church bodies are engaged in negotiations which look toward intercommunion, believing that the time is not ripe for talking of union. And a good many have made their commitments to, and are deepening their participation in, the co-operative efforts of various church councils.

Many of the present denominations are the result of previous unions.[5] Most notable for its embracing of dissimilar churches is the United Church of Canada, formed in 1925 of Congregational, Methodist, and Presbyterian elements. Among other unions now taken for granted are the American Baptist Convention, the Evangelical Lutheran Church, the United Lutheran Church, the American Lutheran Church, the Methodist Church, the Reformed Church, the Evangelical United Brethren, the Congregational-Christian Churches, and the Evangelical and Reformed Church. The last two named have become one body, the United Church of Christ, in 1957.

The union of the United Presbyterian Church and the Presbyterian Church in the U.S.A. is assured for 1958.

Among Lutherans there are two major union movements, and each is expected to be realized within a few years. The American Lutheran Church, the Evangelical Lutheran Church, and the United Evangelical Lutheran Church look forward confidently to their merger in 1960. Also the American Evangelical Lutheran Church, the Augustana Lutheran Church, the Finnish Evangel-

---

[5]cf. Rouse and Neill. *op. cit.* chap. 10 appendix. Also H. P. Douglass, *A Decade of Objective Progress in Church Unity, 1927-36.* Harper and Brothers: New York, 1937; S. C. Neill, *Towards Church Union 1937-1952.* Faith and Order; London, 1952.

ical Lutheran Church, and the United Lutheran Church in America are on their way toward completion of a plan of union.

Meanwhile the Methodist Church and the Protestant Episcopal Church have reached a significant stage of agreement on the terms for intercommunion. And Disciples of Christ have endorsed a plan which, if consummated, would unite seven or eight major denominations as one church.[6] The facts presented to us by these unitive actions of the denominations are a clear demonstration of the degree to which American churches are acting upon the call to unity.[7] Members of these bodies are not asked to express opinions on whether closer unity might in some future time be worthy of consideration. They are faced with the need for decision now; and in most instances the decision is a positive one.

Two observations about these actions are in order. First, let it not be assumed that the merger of two or more denominations is itself the answer to disunity in the Church. The church's unity cannot be isolated from its faith, mission, service, and common life. Therefore an organizational union or administrative merger, which leaves untouched the questions of the essential nature and task of the Church on earth, is only a step in the direction of true unity. In some cases, where there is a calculated indifference to matters of truth in Faith and Order, such merger may actually do injury to Christian unity. This is the reason why the utmost wisdom, prudence, patience, and faith are required to bring about a valid healing of schism.

It is not axiomatic, in the second place, that the goal of these mergers is the eventual union of all American denominations in one *centrally governed* church body. In South India or Ceylon it is perfectly legitimate to favor one single ecclesiastical structure. But it is highly questionable whether the same pattern should be applied in the United States or Canada. The real issue is that of centralized power. The characteristic stance of American Christians respecting liberty and autonomy of churches is incommensurate with the notion of delegating or surrendering excessive administrative authority to a few bishops, executive secretaries, or other ecclesiastical officers. This dread of centralized power, which already is seen in some denominational forms, poses a most intractable

---

[6]cf. Chapter 13 by Charles C. Morrison on the so-called "Greenwich Plan."

[7]For more details, cf. the author's world-wide surveys on church union in *The Ecumenical Review,* April, 1954, October, 1955, and April, 1957.

problem for Christian unity in America. While the pressures for unity drive denominations toward more numerous mergers, thus diminishing the number of denominations, the threat of bureaucratic control increases. The churches then face a choice between the acceptance of a centralized national government, or decentralized regional administration. But regionalism also has its dangers so far as the work and witness of the whole church are concerned. For example, the national character of some denominations has prevented excessive measures being taken by churches of certain regions on the issue of racial segregation and integration. The question remains open but clamors for an answer. Is there an optimum size of a single administrative unit of a united church? Does this suggest a number of autonomous regional churches in America, similar to the territorial *Landeskirchen* of Germany or the cantonal churches of Switzerland? If a risk must be taken, is it better to risk whatever dangers are inherent in regionalism, or those in concentrated authority over a national church? As we face the persistent problem of the goal of the unity movement in America, these questions will become increasingly urgent.

In view of the quite amazing developments of the present century respecting unity, we should not be astonished if even more radical changes take place in the four remaining decades. Attempts at accurate predictions are never taken very seriously. And yet one can now discern a trend toward greater manifestation of church unity which will probably continue without abatement for many years. The still more radical political and social changes of the coming years are almost certain to accelerate the trend. One cannot be so sure of the kind of influence to be exerted by developments in theology and Christian thought, but it is unlikely that the current course of biblical theology and ecumenical concern will have spent its force within a generation or two.

In the final analysis, however, it is scarcely proper for Christians to calculate too carefully what the future may hold for the Church. Believing that unity is a matter of God's gift to the Church, rather than the product of our planning and striving, we acknowledge in faith that it will take the form God intends for it at the time he determines, which means that the highest contribution to be made to the cause of unity is sincere prayer that God's will be done.

Part Two

Christian Unity as God's Will

"... until we all attain to the unity
of the faith ..."

—*Ephesians 4:13*

Chapter Three

Imperatives and Motivations for Church Unity

Roger L. Shinn

Professor of Christian Ethics at the Vanderbilt University
Divinity School; United Church of Christ (from the
Evangelical and Reformed Church)

Christians, like other people, have all kinds of motives. Some of these motives are divisive, some co-operative. If we simply examine our motives, we may find that we want unity or that we prefer disunity.

But we are Christians because we have in some way responded to what God has shown us and has done in Christ. We testify that in Christ, God has reconciled the world unto himself. This testimony is a report, an account of what has happened, an *indicative*. We further testify that God has entrusted to us a ministry of reconciliation. When we accept this trust, we acknowledge an *imperative*. Insofar as we are faithful to the mission given us, our *motives* are no longer just what we happen to feel or will; they are reformed and transformed by God.

Hence our present task is to study the motives for Christian unity and to discover how those *motives* are faithful to God's *imperative* which arises out of God's *indicative*.

I. THE GOSPEL IMPERATIVE TO UNITY

A. Christian Love

The Christian Gospel is the story of God's love. "For God so loved the world that he gave his only Son . . ."

Likewise the imperative coming out of the Gospel is for complete love. When Jesus picks the two great commandments, they

33

concern love for God and love for neighbor. To explain who the neighbor is, Jesus tells the story of the good Samaritan, clearly indicating that the neighbor is not just the person who belongs to "my church" or "my crowd."

The Christian Church has sometimes neglected this part of its faith. Its leaders have at times sought to preserve the purity of the faith by denying love to the infidel and the heretic. But when doctrinal differences destroy love, the Church denies its own Gospel. "He who does not love does not know God; for God is love. . . . if we love one another, God abides in us and his love is perfect in us." (1 John 4:8, 12.)

The very least, then, that Christians may say about church unity is to renounce any form of division that destroys love. It may be that there are forms of organizational difference that do not interfere with love. It is possible that a Presbyterian may love a Baptist without wishing to become a Baptist and without wishing the Baptist to become a Presbyterian. But when churchmanship promotes strife, jealousy, factionalism, it opposes the very meaning of the Gospel which creates the Church.

B. The Community Which Christ Creates

It is not fair to say that the New Testament teaches that Christians should love each other *more* than they love non-Christians. But it does describe a peculiar quality of the love within the Christian community. "A new commandment I give to you, that you love one another; even as I have loved you, that you also love one another. By this all men will know that you are my disciples, if you have love for one another." (John 13:34-35.)

The Church is the community of those called by Christ and responding to him. It does not owe its life to someone's discovery of the abstract idea of love. Rather it exists as a response to God's work in Christ. Hence it sings, "The Church's one foundation is Jesus Christ her Lord." It is not the aggregate of those who agree upon some religious questions and hence decide to start up an organization. Its belief, instead, comes out of a shared experience and a shared loyalty. Writing about the New Testament, Bishop Gustaf Aulén says: "To be a Christian is to be a member of the Church, to have a share in the new *koinōnia*, the New Communion."

Among the many indications that unity is part of the nature of the Church in the New Testament are these:

1. Intrinsic to the meaning of the Church is the idea that God called a people. As Israel was created by God's covenant with a people in the time of Moses, so the Christian Church is the people of the New Covenant. One of the central purposes of revelation was the establishment of this people of God to live under his will.

2. A recurring phrase describing the Church is "the body of Christ." "Now you are the body of Christ and individually members of it." (1 Cor. 12:27.) "Speaking the truth in love, we are to grow up in every way into him who is the head, into Christ, from whom the whole body, joined and knit together by every joint with which it is supplied, when each part is working properly, makes bodily growth and upbuilds itself in love." (Eph. 4:15-16.) Such phraseology does not require that Christians all become alike in all respects; in fact it portrays the maximum of diversity and the maximum of unity at the same time. For, as the various members of the body perform their widely differing functions, they nevertheless belong to the one body, need each other, suffer together, rejoice together.

3. A variety of images in the New Testament express the theme of Christian unity. These include such phrases as "the family of God," "the people of God," "the household of God," "one flock," "the vine and the branches," "the building and the cornerstone." The diversity of the images warns us against basing too much on any single phrase, while the prevalence of the images impresses us with the importance of unity. Some of these phrases express the interpersonal quality of unity more than does "the body of Christ."

4. Christ specifically calls for unity among his followers. He prays that all who shall believe in him may be one, "even as thou, Father, art in me, and I in thee, that they also may be in us, so that the world may believe that thou hast sent me." (John 17:21.) Indeed, the unity of Christ's followers is to be evidence to the world that God has sent Christ.

Thus the call to unity is clarion clear. However, the nature of the unity demanded by this New Testament picture of the Church is debated. There is disagreement among Christians here. Some say that Christ specifically commands one form of organizational and sacramental unity to mediate divine grace to men. Others say that the sort of unity described by the New Testament cannot be guaranteed and can scarcely even be helped by institutional formulas, because it depends on the Spirit.

C. The Christian Witness

The Christian Church is by its nature a witnessing Church. It bears testimony to God in the midst of a world where the powers of evil are rampant. It is commissioned to go into all the world and preach the Gospel to every creature. Because of the nature of evil, that missionary task must always be carried out within the cultures that shelter and patronize the Church as well as in those cultures called pagan.

Some situations dramatize the necessity for a united witness. The army chaplaincy simply cannot be organized on the basis of all the institutional peculiarities of American Christianity. Because the churches want chaplains and because pressures of governmental and military necessity are involved, churches have learned to work together and to share responsibilities.

In foreign missions the same problem is involved. Absence of governmental and military necessity permits duplication and rivalry, but the Gospel imperative remains. We have all heard stories of "Northern" Methodists (or Presbyterians or Baptists) in South China and "Southern" Methodists in North China. In North America there may once have been some sense in having Swedish Lutherans and German Lutherans; but if American missionaries carry such distinctions into Asia, they are bound to feel foolish. Still worse is the bewilderment forced on the man who has heard the new message of Christ and has responded in all sincerity, only to find a second missionary telling him that the first missionary baptized him the wrong way. Out of such experiences the missionary movement has seen that loyalty to Christ demands a united witness to him and has given a new impetus to the ecumenical movement.

Within Christendom the necessity for a united witness is no less, though the excuses for division have a more deceptive plausibility. Since even blatant hostility between churches may not threaten their institutional prosperity in an American city, churches may think they can afford disunity here. But such disunity may be tragic. The churches can hardly exercise their ministry of reconciliation when their own life testifies to unreconciled partisanship.

36

II. Non-Christian Motives for Unity

Our desires for unity do not all come from the Gospel. Some of them, in fact, oppose the Gospel.

A. The Power Cult

In a culture where "bigger" and "better" are almost synonymous, it looks obvious to some people that the church should get into the pattern of American success. General Motors has been a whale of an enterprise, producing several lines of cars within one corporate structure. Why can't the churches do as well? If competition between Chevrolet and Pontiac works so well within the same corporation, why not let the Congregationalists and Episcopalians compete within one big church? The church could then include within itself varieties of doctrine and worship to suit all the potential customers, yet still have the thrill of being one great big church—so big that everyone would have to take notice of it.

How far this spirit of corporate enterprise enters into the desire for church unity is hard to say. Probably it is not a major factor. Yet now and then it is implied in arguments for unity.

Actually this motivation comes out of an ethos that conflicts sharply with the New Testament. The unity it cheers is not the unity which the Gospels describe.

B. Anti-Romanism

The cult of bigness occasionally takes a special form in Protestant rivalry to Roman Catholicism. Sometimes one detects the reasoning: "They all work together; we've got to do the same or they'll get ahead of us." Now and then it seems that the only cause that can draw together some sharply divided Protestant groups is a protest against an ambassador to the Vatican.

Once again this spirit is unworthy of the Gospel. Relations with the Church of Rome involve intricate problems for which no solution is in sight. But when churches that cannot find unity in the Gospel unite to oppose another church, we are far from the unity of love, loyalty, and witness that Christ asks.

C. Tolerance

Another lure of our culture is a kind of tolerance that achieves a sort of unity at too easy a cost. In everyday life many arguments are not worth fighting over. Compromise adjusts differences. The person who will never compromise his interests to accommodate others is antisocial. In an "other-directed society," where conformity is so pervasive a norm, the habit of playing down differences has its practical advantages. In ecclesiastical affairs it becomes easy to say, "Why worry about differences that don't matter? It's much nicer to agree."

This reasoning has its place when differences really do not matter. But when we blithely disregard issues that our forefathers died about, we need to ask why. Perhaps the forefathers were too stubborn and irascible; perhaps we lack the insight and courage to stand by convictions that do matter.

D. Imperialism

But those who resist easy unity, demanding that we come together only on their terms, may be idolizing their own institutions rather than serving Christ. The New Testament repeatedly points out that loyalty to the traditions of men can distort obedience to God.

It is easy to say, "My church is right, yours is wrong. Therefore we can have unity only if yours comes into mine." When many different churches are saying this, some of them (if not all) are by logical necessity wrong.

Imperialism is as tempting as a way to church unity as it is in international affairs. If original sin is pride, one of its deadliest forms is ecclesiastical pride. We recognize it easily in others, but not in ourselves.

It is hard to separate imperialism from an honest witness of faith. For example, take a recent statement by Gustave Weigel, S.J., on the Roman Catholic attitude toward members of other churches. In good faith he says of his own view:

There is no desire to make proselytes after the manner of a political party which wishes to aggrandize itself through numerical increase. Rather there is an altruistic wish to have non-Catholics share in the riches of the Church's dispensation of grace.[1]

Thus, even as he denies the imperialistic approach, we suspect that he may be innocently using a veiled form of it. He, however, can turn the argument back upon us, because he correctly shows that most Protestant approaches to Catholicism, even when offered in spontaneous good faith, really propose that co-operation will be easy if the Catholic will just become a Protestant.

---

[1]"Ecumenism and the Catholic," *Thought*, Spring, 1955, p. 9. Used by permission.

We must keep asking ourselves: Is our desire for unity actually a desire that others become like us, rather than a desire that we, as much as the others, subject ourselves to the Gospel?

III. Christian Motives that May Disrupt

If some motives for unity are sub-Christian, there may be imperatives in the Gospel that interfere with some plans for unity. Jesus and his disciples and apostles, like the Old Testament prophets before them, often disrupted the unity of existing religious institutions.

A. Fidelity

Unity often comes easily to those willing to yield a conviction that others cannot give up. While the New Testament warns against the sin of clinging to human traditions and thereby neglecting God, it also warns against the perils of infidelity. In our time, when American Christianity so easily merges with the prevailing folkways of our culture, we dare not deride those who assert the faith in ways that look peculiar to the world. Many Christians know the Gospel primarily as it comes to them through some specific ecclesiastical tradition. The diversity of these many traditions is both a problem and a challenge to Christians seeking unity. These traditions include forms of church polity (ranging from a specified hierarchy and apostolic succession to thoroughgoing congregational autonomy), beliefs about sacraments (which may demand closed communion or may question the validity of the baptism of some churches), reliance upon specified modes of interpreting Scripture, assertion of certain designated doctrines as utterly essential to the life of the Church.

Some Christians accept one or another of these forms of fidelity; others think the church can include great variety. But all know that fidelity belongs to the life of the Church, that the Church always remains distinctive while it lives. To maintain this Christian distinctiveness against the non-Christian forces of our world is surely a Christian motive. To maintain distinctiveness even against other Christians who easily find pathways to unity may sometimes also be a Christian motive.

It is possible that enthusiasts for Christian unity dismiss resisters too superciliously. To compromise a Christian loyalty for the sake of a sub-Christian agreement is no gain. Opponents of plans for unity *may be* clinging to the Gospel rather than modifying it to join the common accord.

39

B. The Impulse to Reform

One form of fidelity is the impulse to reform. Repeatedly since New Testament times the great church has nurtured reformers in its midst. These reformers usually trouble the equanimity, if not the unity, of the church. Often the reformer is one of the most loyal members of the church, expressing his loyalty by recalling the church to its mission. The church, likewise, accepts the troubling voice from within its own company. But sometimes the church expels its reformers, and sometimes the reformers break with the institutional church.

The very size of the great church may present a problem, for a large church develops massive institutional forms, bureaucracies, modes of accommodation with the world. At such times the "sectarian" ethos, the ethos of "the church against the world," the ethos so prominent in the Book of Acts may lead to severe criticism of the conventional church. Ideally the great church will welcome that criticism from within. But there is always the possibility that such criticism will break the structure of the church.

Some Christians, while seeing the imperative for greater unity in the church today, can imagine a successful unity movement which might stifle the creative minorities. At such a time reform, though it cannot have the purpose of disunity, may unintentionally but necessarily produce disunity. Yet Christians always hope that reform will itself lead to greater unity, and that a united church can constantly encourage reform in its midst.

IV. Ambiguous Motives for Unity

Some motives for unity are ambiguous; that is, a statement of them does not show immediately whether they are responses to the Christian imperative or imports into the Christian message. Their validity depends less upon their formal statement than upon the context in which they are offered.

A. Efficiency

One such motive is efficiency. We frequently hear of the waste and duplicated effort involved in church divisions. Two denominations build churches across the street from each other; by uniting their efforts they could at less cost build a church better than either is now getting. Or two denominations each publish a complete line of literature, whereas they might combine and produce better publications for less money.

40

Such an argument may represent business expediency, the intrusion of the spirit of commercialism into our churches. But it may be a genuinely Christian concern. Truman Douglass writes:

> In some areas of the church's life, to be inexpedient or imprudent is to be unfaithful. The notion that the efficient conduct of the temporal affairs of the churches is a matter of no religious consequence is reflective of a kind of religion so spiritualized and etherealized as to be ethically irresponsible.
>
> If a fellowship of churches, by improving its administrative efficiency, can put larger resources into the work of evangelism, the Christian education of its children, the outreach of its missions, it is being careless of its stewardship, negligent of its accountability to God for the use of its life and strength if it fails to do so.[2]

B. Irrelevance of Old Divisions

A frequent argument for unity is that many sources of denominational division, once important, now have ceased to be real issues. Only the inertia of institutions maintains existing divisions. For instance, in the colonization of America it was natural to establish churches for linguistic groups; now this reason is often outdated, but the old institutions hang on.

If this is an argument for a tidying up of organizations because of a rationalistic desire to eliminate particularities, it is not Christian reasoning. But if it points to the way in which old wounds or dead controversies interfere with a unified witness of the Christian church, it is an implication of the Gospel.

C. Our Need for Each Other

Another persuasive argument for unity is that an ecumenical Church (and to some degree any lesser form of church union) offers the opportunity for the enriching of the common life as many groups bring into it the deposit of their traditions and experiences.

Such a view may be little more than an argument for Pan-American amity on the grounds that coffee and a banana from Latin America improve breakfast. There is a similar dilettante version of religion which enjoys sampling the quaint ways of various groups lest one get jaded by too much of his own.

This motive, however, may show a real awareness of the New Testament description of diversity of gifts with the same Spirit. Thus, for instance, some Americans have gained from the ancient

---

[2]"Great and Honourable Actions . . . Answerable Courages," *Advance,* Sept. 21, 1955. Used by permission.

Mar Thoma Church of India, not the enjoyment of something curiously different but the cleansing experience of meeting a faith which has not become so amalgamated with Western culture that (as in ours) one can scarcely distinguish what is Christ's from what belongs to European and American inventive genius.

D. Response to Crisis

Certainly there is in the ecumenical movement a response to the crisis of our times. Father Weigel in his candidly fascinating study of "Ecumenicism and the Catholic" has confronted us with the problem. The dominance of Protestantism over some sections of culture has been broken, he says, by the rise of secularism, naturalism, and (in some cases) resurgent Roman Catholicism. Hence, he writes:

> The alarm occasioned by these facts has driven the Protestants to plug up anxiously the leaks through which their strength is flowing away. The biggest leak was the splintered multiplicity of churches. The reduction of this multiplicity to some amorphous kind of unity is the World Council. Hence to many a Catholic the World Council is nothing more than "Protestantism, Inc.," in spite of the presence of some Orthodox churches and the absence of such genuinely Protestant groups as the "smaller sects" and the fundamentalists.[3]

Again the situation is ambiguous. The response to the current crisis may be tactical—like that of the football coach who in a tough situation juggles the lineup or tries some new plays. Conceivably the ecumenical movement may be an *ad hoc* adjustment of strategy and no more.

But it has always been the Christian faith that God reveals himself to men in history. The crises of history are times of judgment and renewal. It can be true that the perils of modern history are calling the Church to repentance and renewal, that the ecumenical movement is the response of Christian people to God in awakening devotion.

Thus some churchmen have found in the current American crises of race relations that the very divisiveness of society impresses them with their oneness in Christian faith and purpose. It has often been said in the ecumenical movement that there can be no reunion without renewal. If the Church in these days of the shaking of the nations finds reunion and renewal, then unity will be far more than a strategy for crisis. It will be the Gospel of Christ at work in his Church.

---

[3] *Op. cit.*, p. 10.

Chapter Four

The Biblical Doctrine
of the Church and Its Unity

Theophilus M. Taylor

Professor of New Testament Literature and Exegesis,
Pittsburgh-Xenia Theological Seminary; United Presbyterian Church

I. ANTECEDENTS OF THE 'CHURCH' CONCEPT IN JESUS' TEACHING

Quite consistently with the continuance of the earliest Christian community in the double cult (temple and synagogue) of Judaism, we must note when we come to the life and teaching of Jesus that he himself worshiped in "the synagogue, as his custom was, on the sabbath day," and that he frequented the temple at the festival seasons of the Jewish year as he had been brought up to do. Nor did he ever make the slightest suggestion that his disciples should do otherwise. It is only natural, therefore, that the record in Acts, even though it also notes exclusively Christian gatherings from the very beginning, should indicate the continuing worship of Christians in the regular services of the temple and synagogues.

A. The Use of the Term, *Ekklēsia*

It is also noteworthy that the word *ekklēsia,* perhaps surprisingly to the average Christian, occurs but twice in the Gospels, and that both occurrences are in Matthew. In 16:18 we find the famous "keys of the kingdom" passages, where in response to Peter's confession near Caesarea Philippi, Jesus replied, "You are Peter, and on this rock I will build my church, and the powers of death shall not prevail against it." Again in 18:17 the disciple was advised to try to settle differences with his fellows privately, or in company with a few friends, but in the last resort if he could get nowhere with the offending brother he was advised to "tell it to the church; and if he refuses to listen even to the church," then he should count the offender "as a Gentile and a tax collector."

Realizing that the term *ekklēsia* here has not yet been filled with the nuances characteristic of later Christian usage, we must assume that these two appearances of the word still represented the basically Jewish and Old Testament conception of "congregation" or "assembly" of the people of God. Jesus certainly spoke in Aramaic, a late offshoot of Hebrew, but whether he used the Aramaic cognate for *'edhah* or *qahal* it is now impossible to determine with certainty. Upon the ground of predominant Septuagint usage, the latter would seem to be more likely. In any case these two appearances parallel the later Christian usage which knows only two meanings for *ekklēsia:* (1) the entire body of believers in the world, and (2) any local congregation of believers.

B. The "Kingdom of God" Idea

We are, therefore, driven to look elsewhere for the major antecedent of the concept of "the Church" in the teachings of Jesus. While he had relatively little to say about "the Church," we find Jesus' teaching saturated with references to the "kingdom of God" or the "kingdom of heaven." This is immediately suggestive, particularly when we consider over against it that in the Pauline letters the "kingdom of God" appears relatively infrequently while references to "the Church" abound. For all practical purposes, it is not too much to say that "the kingdom of God," or its equivalent "the kingdom of heaven," is the true and proper correlate of "the Church" in the Gospels. Or, put it the other way round, "the kingdom of God" in transit—in process of growth between its inauguration and its consummation.

The main burden of Jesus' message was "the kingdom of God." Indeed, Mark summarized it by saying, "Jesus came into Galilee, preaching the gospel of God, and saying, 'The time is fulfilled, and the kingdom of God is at hand; repent, and believe in the gospel.' " (1:14-15.) Twice Matthew summarized Jesus' message by declaring, "Jesus went about . . . preaching the gospel of the kingdom." (4:23, 9:35.) In the Synoptic Gospels the phrase

44

"kingdom of God [heaven]" actually occurs in 79 sayings; and they deal with everything from its immediate proximity, the attainment of citizenship in it, and its nature, to its final consummation.

We are here concerned with his conception of its composition, and with whatever implications that conception may have for the development of the proper Christian attitude in areas of human division and tension today. For that reason we limit our discussion to those sayings that have an obvious and immediate bearing on our problem.

It is noteworthy, first of all, that among the prerequisites to kingdom citizenship there are none which are culturally, economically, or racially determined. Contrariwise, the only prerequisite is a right attitude—the attitude of purity and innocence.

"Let the children come to me, do not hinder them; for to such belongs the kingdom of God. Truly, I say to you, whoever does not receive the kingdom of God like a child shall not enter it." (Mark 10:14-15.)

"Unless you turn and become like children, you will never enter the kingdom of heaven. Whoever humbles himself like this child, he is the greatest in the kingdom of heaven." (Matthew 18:3-4.)

"Blessed are the poor in spirit, for theirs is the kingdom of heaven." (Matthew 5:3.)

Such right behavior includes a forgiving spirit[1] and an active social conscience toward the less fortunate among men.[2]

The idea that kingdom citizenship might be the prerogative of a cultural aristocracy, or of Israel as a "chosen race," was deliberately exploded by Jesus. In a speech which the Evangelist said was addressed particularly to "the chief priests and the elders of the people," and "the Pharisees"[3]—that is, to the religious leaders of Judaism, and hence, to then current Judaism itself, Jesus said,

"The kingdom of God will be taken away from you and given to a nation producing the fruits of it." (Matthew 21:43.)

This was a word that must have been a great consolation to the Gentile church in later years. That there is no relationship whatever between a humanly conceived cultural-religious aristocracy

[1]E.g., Matt. 5:7, 24-25, 39-42, 44-45; 6:12, 14-15; 18:23-33, etc.
[2]E.g., Matt. 9:35-36; 10:40-42; 18:5; 25:31-46, etc.
[3]Matt. 21:23, 45.

45

and the divinely recognized "democracy of the spirit" may be seen in the same address to the same audience:

"The tax collectors and the harlots go into the kingdom of God before you. For John came to you in the way of righteousness, and you did not believe him, but the tax collectors and the harlots believed him; and even when you saw it, you did not afterward repent and believe him." (Matthew 21:31-32.)

The material-economic standards of measurement which are nearly always involved in any form of cultural and racial stratification of society may actually be deterrents to kingdom citizenship:

"How hard it will be for those who have riches to enter the kingdom of God!"
"It is easier for for a camel to go through the eye of a needle than for a rich man to enter the kingdom of God." (Mark 10:23, 25.)

Finally, Jesus pronounced a curse on those who would attempt to establish a religious aristocracy:

"Woe to you, scribes and Pharisees, hypocrites! because you shut the kingdom of heaven against men; for you neither enter yourselves, nor allow those who would enter to go in." (Matthew 23:13.)

On the positive side, it is quite clear that all men, all nations, and all strata of human society, are not only eligible for kingdom citizenship, they are to be considered by those who are already citizens as proper prospects for citizenship, and are to be encouraged and urged to become citizens. The earliest Christian community understood this clearly. Matthew's version of the interpretation of the parable of the sower reflects it: "The field [in which the Word is to be sown] is the world." (Matthew 13:38.) The model prayer Jesus suggested to the disciples has it:

"Thy kingdom come,
Thy will be done,
On earth as it is in heaven." (Matthew 6:10.)

It would be impossible not to consider God's kingdom *heaven-wide* in its extent, and if it is to come "on earth as it is in heaven" it must eventuate in an *earth-wide* kingdom. Jesus' summary of the Law, in which love of *neighbor* is put alongside love of God,[4] implied such an eventuality, especially in the light of the explana-

---

[4]Mark 12:29-31.

tion of the term "neighbor" in the story of the good Samaritan involving one of another racial background,[5] and of the admonition, "Love your enemies and pray for those who persecute you [such as tax collectors and *Gentiles*]."[6] The eschatalogical discourse has it where, according to Mark's version, "the gospel must first be preached to all nations" (13:10), or in Matthew's report, "this gospel of the kingdom will be preached throughout the whole *world*" (Gk. *telos,* lit. "consummation"). The various versions of "the great Commission"[7] make it explicit; and the activity of the earliest Christian community as reflected in Acts confirms it beyond any shadow of doubt. Paul understood his personal commission to involve his preaching Christ "among the Gentiles."[8] The good news of the kingdom was understood, from the earliest days of the Church, to be for the whole "inhabited earth," and for all nations resident in it.

C. The "Family" Analogy

We have already seen that Jesus deplored men's profession of his Lordship when it was not accompanied by obedience to God's will: "Not every one who says to me, 'Lord, Lord,' shall enter the kingdom of heaven, but he who does the will of my Father who is in heaven." (Matthew 7:21.) This protest was grounded in the Semitic conception of the family, in which the family is in reality the primary unit in society and possesses a physico-psychic unity involving flesh and blood on the one hand, and an emotional, intellectual, and volitional rapport on the other. The Semitic father is the nucleus of family life; and the family enjoys an inner sense of harmonious wholeness, and functions efficiently in the larger social groupings (such as tribe, nation, or kingdom) only insofar as all its members recognize and support the central, nuclear position of the father.

Jesus, therefore, conceived of the kingdom of God in typically Semitic fashion when he said that those who enter the kingdom of heaven will be those who do the will of their heavenly Father. This family analogy was assumed when Jesus taught his disciples to address God as "Our Father" (Matthew 6:9); and it was further

---

[5]Luke 10:29-37.
[6]Matt. 5:43-48.
[7]Matt. 28:18-20; Luke 24:46-48; Acts 1:8.
[8]Gal. 1:15-16.

47

drawn out when, upon being told that his own mother and brothers wished to speak with him, he replied, "Who are my mother and my brothers?" Then, looking about at his disciples who were present, he added, "Here are my mother, and my brothers! Whoever does the will of God is my brother, and sister, and mother." (Mark 3:33-35.)

But this "kingdom of God" family is on a supra-flesh-and-blood level, for those whose decisions to follow Jesus cut them off from their immediate families were assured by him:

"There is no one who has left house or brothers or sisters or mother or father or children or lands, for my sake and for the gospel [of the kingdom], who will not receive a hundredfold now in this time, houses and brothers and sisters and mothers and children and lands, with persecutions, and in the age to come eternal life." (Mark 10:29-30.)

Here it is clear that the family fellowship of the disciples in their new kingdom of God relationship was to be so intimately real that it would properly substitute for the losses they might incur in being cut off from their own flesh and blood.

Professor Jacques Ellul was on perfectly safe ground, then, when he wrote:

We should have a great deal to do, therefore, first of all by way of education, and then in practice, to teach Christians that they belong to Christ before their country, that everything is God's and must be rendered unto Him, that only *after* this total gift has been made have they the right to render anything to Caesar. They must learn that a *French Christian is, because he is a Christian first and foremost, more closely linked to a German Christian than to a French non-Christian.* It is absolutely vital to create in this way an international (I would say, "supranational") Christian attitude of mind.[9]

His statement may be extended upon the basis of Jesus' teaching in many other directions. For instance, it is urgent that white Christians be given to understand that, in the mind of Christ, they are, because they belong to the family of God first and foremost, more closely related to the Negro, Indian, Chinese, and Japanese Christians than they are to white non-Christians. Conversely, Negro Christians ought to feel a closer kinship to white or other kinds of Christians than to Negro non-Christians. Indeed, it is

---

[9]*The Ecumenical Review.* April, 1952, p. 274. Used by permission.

not too much to say that, upon the basis of Jesus' teaching, I, as a white Christian, ought to feel a closer relationship to my fellow Christians of another race than I do toward a member of my own immediate family who is not a Christian.

This is true because relationships within the family of God are found at a deeper level than those resulting from the mere accidents of human parenthood. We cannot forget in this connection the warning of John the Baptist to his contemporary fellow countrymen:

"Do not presume to say to yourselves, 'We have Abraham as our father'; for I tell you, God is able from these stones to raise up children to Abraham." (Matthew 3:9.)

The ability to demonstrate a pure Hebrew bloodline in one's ancestry was a false premise upon which to claim to be God's children. Rather, a life in which "fruits befitting repentance" could be seen—this was the proper identification of God's true offspring.

D. The Temple: Symbol for the Congregation of Israel

One more element pointing toward the later conception of the Church remains to be considered in the teaching of Jesus. This is the figure of the temple. Even though the synagogues had by the first century achieved an ineradicable position of importance in Jewish life, never again to be eclipsed by the temple, it is still true the Herodian temple in Jerusalem remained a great visible symbol of the over-all oneness of Jewish religion. In a particular way it signalized the unity of those who revered the law of the world. Thus the temple, which in the Israelite monarchy had taken the place of the earlier temporary and movable tabernacle and to which in pre-exilic times all males were expected to report for the great festival occasions of the Jewish religious year, continued to be the symbol of the gathered "congregation of Israel."

It is significant, therefore, that upon the occasion of his cleansing the temple, Jesus should have characterized the ideal temple of God by a sentence drawn from the Scriptures of his own people: " 'My house shall be called a house of prayer for all the nations.' "[10] This quotation from the Septuagint (Greek) version of Isaiah was well chosen by Jesus both for its contextual setting, and for its inherent possibilities of meaning. It occurs in the midst of a para-

---

[10]Mark 11:17.

49

graph which has unmistakably in mind the gathering of dispersed Judaism,[11] *together with*

". . . foreigners who join themselves to the LORD,"[12]

". . . yet others . . . besides those already gathered."[13]

Thus it was in truth "a house of prayer for *all* nations [or people]."

There is, in addition, a wealth of meaning intrinsic to the language of the phrase itself. For one thing the word translated "house" (Heb. *bayith, beyth*) is capable of more than one meaning. Thus in this usage it could apply equally to the physical temple ("house" in the sense of "a building"), and to the people of God ("house" in the sense of "family"). Moreover, the entire phrase, "house of prayer" (Heb. *beyth tepillah*—Gk. *oikos proseuches*), had, by the time Jesus employed it, become one of the common Jewish designations for a synagogue. And "synagogue," in turn, indicated primarily a congregation of God's people gathered for prayer, and secondarily the building in which they so met. We see, therefore, the singular appropriateness of the Isaiah passage for Jesus' purpose. The temple or place of worship, ideally considered, was a building dedicated to the business of prayer, and open to all comers; and the congregation of God's people, symbolized by the temple, was to be a family drawn from all nations and dedicated to prayer (worship).

The significance of this word about the temple for the later conception of "the Church" is, therefore, quite apparent. It is corroborative, on the one hand, of the lack of culturally or racially determined prerequisites to kingdom citizenship (church membership), and on the other hand of the positive concept of a kingdom (Church) which is avowedly from the start intended to be multiracial and multinational. Here was a word attributed by the prophet to God himself. Jesus took it as an epitome of the divine will for the house of God, considered both as the place where worship was to occur and as the assembly of his people who were to worship therein.

Without begging the question as to how fully aware Jesus was, at the moment, of the long centuries of history stretching out

[11]Isaiah 56:8a.
[12]Isaiah 56:6a.
[13]Isaiah 56:8a.

before his "congregation" or "church," it is obvious from his application of this prophetic word to the situation immediately at hand that he did not apply it to some distant eschatological realization. Rather, it was applied to the temple as a symbol of the worshiping assembly of God's people at the beginning of its New Testament manifestation. It seems highly probable that Jesus continued to think of those whom he called to repentance, as composing "the eschatological congregation" of the last days. But "the last days" were upon them. They were living in the midst of them. The multiracial, multinational character of Christ's Church was, therefore, in the mind of its Founder and Head, something to be immediately realized, and henceforth maintained. There was certainly no place in his mind for its postponement to "a more convenient season."

II. THE CHURCH IN PAULINE THEOLOGY

While it is possible to make tentative reconstructions of the emerging conception of the Church in the pre-Pauline era, it was in the theology of Paul that the conception found its fullest New Testament expression, and all that is said of it in the later parts of the New Testament are either mere repetitions, or modest developments erected upon the Pauline baseline. We therefore conclude our paper with a study of the Church in the Pauline context.

A. Only Two Uses of *Ekklēsia* in Paul

We have already intimated in the introduction of our paper that the substitution of *ekklēsia* for *synagogē* probably first took place in the Hellenistic Christian synagogues with which Paul seems from the first to have been most closely associated. We have also pointed out that Matthew is the only Gospel to employ the term, *ekklēsia,* and that the two occurrences (16:18; 18:17) parallel the later Christian usage which recognizes only two meanings. The term, which occurs about 70 times in the Pauline corpus, is always used either (1) of the entire body of Christ—the Church catholic,[14] or (2) of local congregations.[15] This reflects first-century Jewish usage, which, as we have seen, recognized the temple as a symbol

---

[14]E.g., 1 Cor. 10:32; 11:22; 12:28; 15:9; Gal. 1:13; Col. 1:18, 24; Eph. 1:22f.; 2:10, 21; 5:23-32.
[15]E.g., 1 Thess. 1:1; 2:14; 1 Cor. 1:2; 4:17; 11:16, 18; 14:4, 23, 33; 16:1, 9; Gal. 1:2, 22, etc.

of the entire body of Judaism, "the congregation of God," and at the same time had become accustomed to thinking of the local synagogue as a local "congregation," which indeed the Greek term *synagogē* signified. In this sense, both temple and synagogue must be reckoned in the ancestry of the Christian Church; and we shall see that the Pauline conception of the Church is built upon both.

B. The Pauline Conception of the Church Sociologically Conditioned

Any thoroughgoing study of the Pauline conception of the Church soon discovers that it is, in its entirety, conditioned by Semitic sociological assumptions and considerations. In this respect it builds upon the foundations laid by Jesus who proclaimed the presence of the kingdom of God conceived in basically patriarchal terms in which God is at once Father and King, and the citizens of the kingdom are at once family and subjects, who do the Father-King's will. Every figure used of the Church in the Pauline writings is drawn from Semitic anthropology or sociology (the two fields of thought were not sharply distinguishable) and can be so demonstrated.

C. The Family Analogy Again

Paul employs the typically Old Testament terminology to refer to the community of God's people. In Galatians 6:15-16, in a context in which he insists that "neither circumcision counts for anything, nor uncircumcision, but a new creation," he speaks of "all who walk by this rule," evidently Christians of both Jewish and Gentile backgrounds, as "the Israel of God." In the same category we should place "the people of God" (Gk. *laos theou*),[16] "the children of God" (Gk. *tekna theou*),[17] and "the sons of God" (Gk. *huioi theou*),[18] all of which designations, having had Septuagint origins, are applied by Paul to the Christian community.

His insistence that the children of Abraham by faith, rather than his blood descendants, are his true descendants and inheritors, is well known.

---

[16]2 Cor. 6:16; Rom. 9:25f.; 11:1f.
[17]Rom. 8:16f., 21; 9:7f.
[18]Gal. 4:6f.; 2 Cor. 6:18; Rom. 8:14, 19, 29; 9:26.

The promise to Abraham and his descendants, that they should inherit the world, did not come through the law but through the righteousness of faith. If it is the adherents of the law who are to be the heirs, faith is null and the promise is void.

That is why it depends on faith, in order that the promise may rest on grace and be guaranteed to all his descendants—not only to the adherents of the law but also to those who share the faith of Abraham, for he is the father of us all. (Romans 4:13-14, 16.)

This position, exegetically based on the Torah, or books of the law, supports the position taken by Jesus that God's "house" is to be "a house of prayer for all the nations" which he based exegetically in the Prophets. We can also see a parallel between Jesus' insistence, on the one hand, that membership in the family depends not upon flesh-and-blood relationships but upon doing the will of the Father, and Paul's assertion, on the other hand, that sharing the faith of Abraham, which is quite as possible for Gentiles as for Jews, is the only requisite to membership in the family of God's people.

Indeed, God had counted Abraham righteous on the basis of his faith before he was circumcised, which, Paul reasons, was specifically so that Abraham should be "the father of all who believe without being circumcised and who thus have righteousness reckoned to them, and likewise the father of the circumcised who are not merely circumcised but also follow the example of the faith [of Abraham]." (Romans 4:11-12.) Thus both Jesus and Paul flatly deny that racial, or flesh-and-blood relationships of any kind are determinative of membership in God's family. Paul, too, then, supports the supraracial, supranational character of kingdom citizenship (church membership).

It should, perhaps, be pointed out here that Jesus' phrasing of the primary requirement, "Whoever does the will of God" (Mark 3:35), and Paul's phrasing of it, "it depends on faith" (Romans 4:16), are not in any sense opposed to one another. One of the insights for which current Pauline scholarship is greatly indebted to Rudolf Bultmann is his demonstration that faith (Gk. *pistis*) for Paul is never divorced from obedience. Paul's violent objection to a righteousness based on works is not in conflict with the Christian's responsibility to be obedient to the will of God. The word "faith" (*pistis*) in Paul's letters, therefore, should always be thought of as "faith-obedience." Conversely, in the Gospels, obedience to God's will is never considered outside the context of faith—belief in God and a consequent acceptance of his standards.

D. The Temple Symbolism Again

Paul also employs another figure, for which there is precedent in the teaching of Jesus, but he gives it a slightly different thrust. We have seen that the Herodian temple was the object of religious pilgrimage for Jews from all over the world and that, as such, it symbolized the unity of dispersed Judaism. When Jesus cleansed it of its merchants and moneychangers, he quoted words of God revealed to the prophet in Isaiah 56:7 which could be held to refer both to the physical temple and the assembly of its worshipers. God's "house" was in either case "a house [Gk. *oikos*] of prayer for all the nations." The main thrust here seems to be that it is specifically designed so as to comprehend all nations. When, however, addressing the saints who composed the church at Corinth, Paul said, "Do you not know that you are God's temple [Gk. *naos*] and that God's Spirit dwells in you?" in 1 Corinthians 3:16, we see a different emphasis reflected.

This is a notion which can be understood only against Paul's conception of the Church as the body of Christ, and of baptism as the normal act of incorporation into that body.

For just as the body is one and has many members, and all the members of the body, though many, are one body, so it is with Christ. For by one Spirit we were all baptized into one body—Jews or Greeks, slaves or free— and all were made to drink of one Spirit. (1 Corinthians 12:12-13.)

The central Pauline figure for the Church—the body of Christ— we have yet to discuss. But for our immediate purposes it suffices to note that Paul uses the term "temple" (Gk. *naos*, literally "sanctuary," the *cella*, or *sekos*) of the corporate worshiping community itself.

Together they compose *naos theou*, "temple of God." This is not symbolism so much as it is an explicit equation. Here they are the *naos*, the temple, the house of God.

Now we must get the whole "temple" passage before us:

Do you not know that you are God's temple and that God's Spirit dwells in you? If any one destroys God's temple, God will destroy him. For God's temple is holy, and that temple you are. (1 Corinthians 3:16-17.)

54

Paul did not say the Corinthian church is *"the* temple of God" (Gk. *ho naos tou theou*), but that it is "God's temple" (*naos theou*). The temple *in toto* can be equated only to the Church *in toto*. Yet the Christian community in Corinth is part of the whole, and thus can be said to be "God's temple," and each saint (holy, or sanctified person), or member of the church, partakes in that temple. By his baptism he was injected into the body of Christ, and by his baptism he was made to drink of one Spirit. (See 1 Corinthians 12:13.) This is his charter to participation in the temple of God. Indeed, Paul can also speak of the individual saint's body as "a temple of the Holy Spirit," and declare that it is his obligation "to glorify God in [his] body." (1 Corinthians 6:19-20.) In this kind of reasoning anthropological and sociological conceptions of the church are merged. What makes a temple a temple is that it is a residence of the deity; and all Christians, regardless of the individual differences, being corporately bound up in the one body of Christ, compose the temple in which God dwells through his Spirit.

E. The Central Pauline Conception: The Church as Body of Christ

There can be no question that the ranking conception of the Church in the Pauline corpus is the conception of it as the body of Christ. We have already been prepared for this in our consideration of the Church as a temple, a notion erected upon the same kind of foundation. But in this case Paul worked it out much more elaborately. Each Christian upon his baptism not only drinks of the one Spirit, but is granted certain spiritual gifts[19] individually by the Spirit as he wills. Of these he is a steward under God for the edification of the Church. In this respect each Christian may be compared to the individual members or parts of the physical body, each of which is designed for, and is expected to fulfill, a particular function for the benefit of the entire person. So, Paul says, "God has so adjusted the body, . . . that there may be no discord in the body, but that the members may have the same care for one another." (1 Corinthians 12:24b-25.)

The only differences noted between Christians are in the gifts given by the Spirit to each one, and all are equally of value for the total life of the body. Even the most modest gifts are indis-

---

[19]Designated as *pneumatika,* 1 Cor. 12:1, Rom. 1:11, or *charismata,* 1 Cor. 12:4.

pensable, and the body functions properly as a whole only when each member performs, harmoniously with the others, the functions expected of it. There are no economic, educational, national, racial, or social distinctions among them, but only differences of function within the body. They are all expected to be in the body and to work harmoniously together for the good of the body and its head, who is Christ.[20]

As a matter of fact, cultural differences of all kinds are to be expected among Christians, the individual members of Christ's body, the Church. "There is neither Jew nor Greek, there is neither slave nor free, there is neither male nor female; for you are all one in Christ Jesus." (Galatians 3:28.) This was certainly to be expected quite as much in any local congregation as in the whole body of Christ, the Church universal. There is no suggestion anywhere that the church at Ephesus, for instance, should be only for Greeks and the one at Corinth only for Jews, or that the church at Philippi was exclusively for merchants and government officials while that at Thessalonica was for mechanics and day laborers.

The most notable cultural difference of the day was that between Jew and Gentile, yet even this difference was to be erased in the Christian community so that no trace of it remained. The Ephesian letter makes this quite explicit. Gentiles, nicknamed by Judaism "the uncircumcised" and hence considered as the epitome of a depraved and defiled condition, once "separated from Christ, alienated from the commonwealth of Israel, and strangers to the covenants of promise," have been brought near by the sacrificial atonement of Christ. Both Jew and Gentile have, thus, been made one, and the old divisive hostilities have been removed. (See Ephesians 2:12-22.)

The purpose of the atonement itself was, as expressed in Ephesians:

that [Christ] might create in himself one new man in place of the two [Jew and Gentile], so making peace, and might reconcile [them] both to God in one body through the cross, thereby bringing the hostility to an end. (2:15-16.)

---

[20]Implied in 1 Cor. 12:27; explicit in Col. 1:18, 24; Eph. 1:22f.

56

Surely we are to reason that if in the first century Jew and Gentile could be reconciled by Christ "in one body through the cross," the racial and cultural differences of the twentieth century can, and should, also be reconciled through the cross.

Paul had expressed substantially the same note in 2 Corinthians:

> If any one is in Christ, he is a new creation; the old one has passed away, behold, the new has come. All this is from God, who through Christ reconciled us to himself and gave us the ministry of reconciliation; that is, God was in Christ reconciling the world to himself, not counting their trespasses against them, and entrusting to us the message of reconciliation. So we are ambassadors for Christ, God making his appeal through us. (5:17-20.)

The Christian, by virtue of his own reconciliation to God through Christ, has become a new creature, and as such has been granted by God a ministry and a message of reconciliation for all men. It is through the Christian that God continues to make his appeal to a lost world—to lost men. This is a profound truth that has far-reaching implications for the Christian and his attitude toward others. If the God "who did not spare his own Son but gave him up for us all" (Romans 8:32) intends to make his appeal to a lost world through the Christian, it should certainly follow that the Christian must demonstrate something like God's self-sacrifice. It will not be enough to be reconciled to Christians of different racial and cultural backgrounds *after* we meet them as brothers in the Church. We must remember that "God shows his love for us in that *while we were yet sinners* Christ died for us." (Romans 5:8.)

The Christian, if he is to be Christ's ambassador and the agent through whom God makes his appeal to men, must demonstrate a similar love—a love which extends to men while they are still unrepentant sinners, and *before* they have been reconciled to God. This is redemptive love in the highest sense.

Any denial that racial and cultural differences can be blotted out in the Christian community, whether by assertion or by the practices of the church, is tantamount to a denial, by those who make it, of the power and efficacy of the atonement. Or it is probably more accurate to say that their acceptance of the atonement and their experience of the reconciliation it is intended to effect is woefully deficient.

III. Conclusion

From our study, it becomes apparent that the Church, which is the present historical manifestation of the kingdom of God, has but one requirement for membership: that one should do the will of God and accept Christ's righteousness by faith. This may sound like two requirements but they are really one. The Church, moreover, is specifically designed as a house for all nations, and for all the categories of society—Jew and Greek, slave and freeman, male and female. As such it is supranational and supraracial. In it men of the most widely varied backgrounds, finding themselves reconciled to God, discover themselves also reconciled to one another. More than that, they discover that God has granted to them a message and a ministry of reconciliation in behalf of all mankind. "God was in Christ reconciling the world to himself, . . . and entrusting to us the message of reconciliation." (2 Corinthians 5:19.) This reconciliation which Christians claim, if it has been truly effective, results in the destruction of all the old hostilities based on racial and cultural differences. Indeed, Christians discover that they have, in the church, bonds of brotherhood which transcend the flesh-and-blood bonds of ordinary human kinship. They find themselves more closely bound to Christians of differing racial or cultural backgrounds than they do to non-Christians within their own immediate families. And in their fellowship in the Christian community they compose the body of Christ, each receiving certain spiritual gifts from the Spirit of God for the building up, or edifying, of the entire body. In this fellowship they also discover that "If one member suffers, all suffer together; [but] if one member is honored, all rejoice together." (1 Corinthians 12:26.)

Upon the basis of these conclusions with regard to the whole Church of Jesus Christ, we may reason that each congregation, as a local manifestation of it, should reflect the same general characteristics. If the Church is, in its Lord's own mind, "a house of prayer for all the nations," it ought early in its history to begin to reflect the fact. In the early Church which was confident that its Lord had commissioned it to be his "witnesses in Jerusalem and in all Judea and Samaria and to the end of the earth" (Acts 1:8), we find a working out of this, its Lord's design for it. On the same basis a local congregation ought to feel obligated to share the

58

message of reconciliation with the entire cross section of the community in which it is located. That is to say, it should consider the community with all the economic, educational, racial, and cultural strata therein represented as its legitimate field for evangelization. And if it is reasonably faithful in its evangelistic task, it should not be long before such a congregation would begin to reflect within itself an approximate cross section of its home community. By the same token when the community cross section changes in any way, such changes, whether racial, cultural, or economic, should be shortly reflected in the cross section of the congregational membership. Where churches fail to reflect these changes, and become "closed corporations," catering to particular cultural, economic, or racial strata in society, they are already denying the efficacy of the atonement in their own life, and thus undermining the effectiveness of the very Gospel they seek to proclaim.

People, no matter who they are, know when they aren't wanted. How can the Gospel of him who said, "Come to me, all who labor and are heavy-laden" (Matthew 1128), be proclaimed from a church which in effect says, No day laborers, no beggars, no down-and-outers, no Negroes, no Puerto Ricans, no Mexicans, no sharecroppers, no "Oakies" wanted here?

Chapter Five

The Unity Christ Sustains

Carl F. H. Henry

Editor of *Christianity Today;* American Baptist Convention

I.

One of the New Testament ideals is Christian unity (*henōtes*) — the unity of the Spirit and of the faith. (Ephesians 4:3, 13.)

Whoever meditates upon our Lord's high priestly prayer cannot escape the conviction that division and fissure in the body of Christ thwart the Redeemer's prayer and constitute a grievous sin. Among the prime objectives for which believers are to be specially kept or preserved is an existence in unity: "Keep them . . . that they may be one." (John 17:11.)

The wickedness of division and schism among believers is enforced by the salutation "*Holy* Father," this being the lone occurrence of this epithet.

The value of Christian unity, and the sinfulness of disunity among believers, is set forth in the further emphasis that contention and schism among the followers of Christ obscure the world's conviction of the Savior's divine mission, and the evidence that believers are special objects of divine love: "that they may become perfectly one, so that the world may know that thou hast sent me and hast loved them even as thou hast loved me." (17:23; cf. v. 21.)

Our Lord's prayer is thus the upper side of the biblical injunction for the unity of the body of Christ. Hence Paul beseeched the Ephesians to endeavor "to maintain the unity of the Spirit in the bond of peace. There is one body, and one Spirit, just as you were called to the one hope that belongs to your call, one Lord, one faith, one baptism, one God and Father of us all, who is above all and through all and in all." (4:3-6.)

No single historical movement holds the necessary potential for actualizing the unity of the body of Christ visibly and organizationally in the twentieth century or any other. Any movement which endeavors to do this is foredoomed to disappointment and therefore to parochialism. The endeavor to manifest the body visibly and temporally in the name of the whole can succeed only in exhibiting a part of the whole. The more this part is dogmatically affirmed to represent the whole, the more it becomes provocative and self-assertive. The reason is threefold.

One is that the unity of the body of Christ exists even while large groups of believers and churches and whole denominations remain outside a visible interchurch organization. Who could assert that multitudes of Southern Baptists, or of Missouri Synod Lutherans, or others of the 15,000,000 American Protestants not represented by any superdenominational agency, would belong for the first time, or more securely, to the body of Christ by joining some such earthly organization?

Another reason is that the visible churches in history are not infallibly composed of believers. Especially is this true in an era of ecclesiastical revolt against the very actuality of special revelation and redemption. Any organization of visible churches must compound this ambiguity.

But a further reason is most decisive. The body of Christ includes believers not only of all nations and races, but of all ages. The communion of the saints is not restricted to any one generation.[1] The unity Christ sustains in his followers is universal and comprehensive, and the manifested body of Christ will be fragmented—the saints of the past in heaven, the present saints on earth, the future saints unborn—with the Second Advent.

And yet our Lord's high priestly prayer doubtless has a special view to the unity of the believers in the world: "And now I am no more in the world, but they are in the world, and I am coming to thee. Holy Father. . . ." (17:11.) For the dead in Christ, who assuredly belong to the body, the disunity of believers is no problem. For that reason the burden of the prayer for oneness

[1]The doctrine of prayers to the dead is, of course, an unnecessary and unscriptural superimposition upon this fact.

61

may be directed toward an achievement by each generation of the maximal historical expression of the unity it has in view.

In the reach for fulfillment, everything depends upon the manner of approach. ". . . The unity we seek" is already a subbiblical and non-Christocentric orientation of the nature of Christian fellowship. Its biblical-evangelical antithesis is "the unity Christ sustains."

Negatively, it is possible to analyze the concepts "seek," "we," and "unity," in order to exhibit what is objectionable in them, and why in this formula they imply already what, at best, promises only a carefully concealed disunity. Positively, it is necessary to develop the biblical alternative since not any and every alternative will do.

Both the high priestly prayer and the larger New Testament exclude the identification of the Christian ideal in terms either of organizational union or of independency. These represent the perilous false antitheses, which an adequate concept of Christian unity transcends. Each has its characteristic error. Organizational union—man sought—looks for a concrete, authoritative manifestation of the body in the present historical order. Independency—man sought—looks for the absolute purity of the local church in the present historical order. The former neglects the purity of the Church and espouses an objectionable form of union; the latter neglects the spiritual unity of Christians as enunciated in the concept that believers are members of one body and espouses an objectionable form of separatism. Both misconceive the true interrelation of the churches in their present situation in life. Both ignore the unity Christ sustains.

It is unnecessary in this context to develop the perils of separatism because the present climate of discussion is contraseparatism and prounion. All that is needed is the observation that if contraseparatist forces tend to operate with an inadequate doctrinal basis, contraunion forces tend to insist upon an excessive basis. The one blithely snips away, e.g., from the Apostles' Creed, which of all theological symbols would appear to have a supreme right to be justly called ecumenical, everything but the thesis that Jesus Christ is Lord and Savior; the other dogmatically appends to it problematical doctrinal affirmations around which the whole climate of theology is made to turn. The one reserves the profoundest eccleciastical recognition and fellowship for the zone of doctrinal deficiency, the other for the zone of doctrinal excess. In this respect, both views depart from the inspired Scriptures as the only criterion of sound doctrine.

Is Christianity prounion or proseparatist? It is both and neither. The church is anti-*oikoumenē;* it is not ecumenically identified. In none of the fifteen New Testament occurrences is the term *oikoumenē* equated with the church, but rather with the world to which the church witnesses.[2] Yet the church can scarcely be called pro-*aphorismos,* proseparatist, on the basis of the lone passage in which that term occurs.

"Therefore come out from them,
and be separate from them, says the Lord,
and touch nothing unclean;
then I will welcome you." (2 Corinthians 6:17.)

This passage deals primarily, as the context makes clear, with separation from the worshipers of idols, not with the basis of Christian unity.[3] On the basis of no passage in the New Testament can the church essentially be characterized either as pro-*oikoumenē* or as pro-*aphorismos.*

II.

More important than emotional reaction to the popular clichés by which the options are today often represented—i.e., the ecumenicists, the separatists—is a critical evaluation of the respective positionizing concepts, and an awareness of the perils they involve.

The one approach sins easily against truth; it tends to cultivate tolerance on the basis of theological relativism, and soon becomes intolerant of revealed theology. The other sins easily against love; it tends to cultivate positive theology on a platform of animosity,

---

[2]The New Testament emphasis is that the gospel is preached for a witness to the *oikoumenē* (Matt. 24:14), that Satan tempted Christ with the kingdoms of the *Oikoumenē* (Luke 4:5), that the apostles were credited with turning the *oikoumenē* upside down (Acts 17:6), that Christ will ultimately judge the *oikoumenē* (17:31), that the *oikoumenē* worships false gods (19:27), that Satan deceives the whole *oikoumenē* (Rev. 12:9), and so forth.

[3]That the New Testament concept of unity is not separatism is apparent from the fact that the Spirit binds all believers together. If organizational union dethrones the centrality of the Spirit among believers, no less does separatism. The body loses its manifested unity as much when it is arbitrarily identified only with a local and independent work as when it is lost in the *oikoumenē,* or equated with some colossal earthly organization. Both sectarian schism and superchurch schematization are kindled by false fires. The Spirit's indwelling places the believer in an internal relation of spiritual oneness with every other believer. Dissolution of this bond, through dissension and party spirit, is a sin against the Holy Spirit. The world thinks the sundered Christian community to be replete with discrepancies and differences, and lacking all real unity.

63

and soon becomes tolerant of lovelessness. Both are sins against Christ.

Say what one will, however, about the terms "ecumenical" and "separatist," it cannot be gainsaid that the visible body of Christ is at once both universal and exclusive. It is not merely local, but world-wide or catholic. Yet, while "in the world," it is not "of the world," but must stand guard against apostasy. Neglect of these distinctives can only result in the merging of objectionable antitheses: the body appears fractured and fragmented, or the world enters the church, and the church becomes the world, and thereby the identity of the body is blurred.

A primary issue today is posed by the question: Where must the line be drawn which marks off church and world in terms of Christian fellowship and unity? That some line must be drawn is nowhere denied in professing Christian circles. The difference between interchurch councils, associations, and fellowships today is not that some draw no line while others insist upon a line. The prime difference concerns where the division is to be made.

The World Council of Churches, despite its widely criticized theological inclusivism, recognizes that some groups are not true churches, excluding them from membership (e.g., Hindus, Moslems, Jehovah's Witnesses, Universalists, and Unitarians). Admittedly, some World Council leaders, such as former president G. Bromley Oxnam, consciously strive for organizational union with the Roman Catholic Church, although the Protestant Reformers declared that church apostate.[4] Others, uncommitted to organizational union with Rome, seek to concretize and institutionalize the Protestant movement on an organizational basis whose theology is inclusivistic. This relative indifference to doctrinal verities within the World Council is one of the cardinal grounds of dissatisfaction among its many critics. The issue is not whether denominational distinctives are often secondary, and provide no genuine barrier to a larger fellowship and co-operation of believers. Rather, it is what significance is to be attached to revealed doctrine in those fundamental matters taught by the Scriptures and recognized by the ecumenical creeds since the earliest centuries of Christian history. Today indifference to revealed doctrine, lamentable enough under any circumstances, is often

---

[4] If the Reformers were incorrect, the very existence of Protestant churches could only be negated, and the World Council of Churches disbanded and its membership returned to the Roman fold.

correlated with a doubt or denial that God has revealed any doctrines at all (in which event it would seem difficult to maintain the thesis that ecumenicity rests upon the revealed will of God).

The liberal Protestant mood has fluctuated between two positions in its repudiation of biblical revelation. Both positions regard doctrinal distinctions as unimportant considerations for church unity. One is "tolerant" even of proponents of dogmatic theology on the grounds of metaphysical scepticism. The other is intolerant of evangelical theology on the ground of speculative metaphysical gnosticism.

The latter position provides the curious spectacle of an inclusivistic exclusivism—the repudiation of revealed theology as an intolerable heresy, and the acceptance of speculative philosophy as "Christian thought."

The Christian Century climaxed the revolt of liberal theology against revealed biblical theism in an editorial asserting that liberals and evangelicals worship not the same God but two different Gods.[5] Could one or the other of these groups then fail to be guilty of idolatry? Must not the possibility of an apostasy of churches and denominations then be admitted even from the perspective of liberalism? Or, if liberalism hoped to avoid intolerance of specially revealed theism (which *The Christian Century* likened to Confucianism in its perversion of genuine Christianity), must it not affirm that it makes no difference how God—or any of the other distinctives of the Christian revelation—is intellectually discriminated?

Does it make any essential difference to the evangelical, whether his confident proclamation of biblically revealed theism is confronted by an intolerant liberal repudiation on the ground of speculative anti-Christian dogmatism, or by tolerant liberal scepticism on the ground of speculative anti-Christian relativism?

---

[5]"Two worlds have clashed, the world of tradition and the world of modernism. . . . There is a clash here as profound and as grim as that between Christianity and Confucianism. Amiable words cannot hide the differences. 'Blest be the tie' may be sung until doomsday but it cannot bind these two worlds together. The God of the fundamentalist is one God; the God of the modernist is another. The Christ of the fundamentalist is one Christ; the Christ of the modernist is another. The Bible of fundamentalism is one Bible; the Bible of modernism is another. The church, the kingdom, the salvation, the consummation of all things—these are one thing to fundamentalists and another thing to modernists. Which God is the Christian God, which Christ is the Christian Christ, which Bible is the Christian Bible, which church, which kingdom, which salvation, which consummation . . . ? The future will tell. But that the issue is clear and that the inherent incompatibility of the two worlds has passed the stage of mutual tolerance is a fact concerning which there hardly seems room for any doubt." ("Fundamentalism and Modernism: Two Religions," an editorial in *The Christian Century*, Vol. XLI, No. 1, Jan. 3, 1924, p. 6.) Used by permission.

To evangelical Christians, the doctrinal indifference of ecumenical inclusivism appears to exclude any genuine basis for unity in essentially Christian dimensions. The separatist movement has pressed the *aphorizo*-concept (2 Corinthians 6:17) on the ground that a denomination becomes apostate, and its churches idolatrous, when its leadership forces men to sin contrary to conscience (e.g., by compelling their support of an inclusivistic theology as a mark of denominational acceptability).

The Corinthian passage, to which the separatist appeals, is not an explicit declaration of Scripture dealing primarily with the apostasy of churches or denominations. The risk involved in an inference from passages of this kind is illustrated by the Millerites, who thought they found in the terrible picture of Babylon, and the call "Come out of her, my people" (Revelation 18:4), a condemnation of the established churches.

When does the preliminary invasion of the church by the world change the integral nature of the church? The separatists propose an answer: when the church forces men, against divine law and conscience, to commit sin. In that event, the church ceases to be a church; it becomes apostate.

The problem of the separatist is that of being certain when a church has become apostate. The conditions which led to the Reformation were several centuries in the making. When does the policy of a shifting majority become the fixed determinate policy, implementing error, disciplining and suspending those who refuse to comply, and holding no prospect of reversal? The separatist asks in turn, How long should we be forced to sin before it becomes sinful? Can any defense of sinning be made?

An intermediary position is asserted. Its emphasis is that while apostasy is doubtless sinful, no church in history has ever been completely pure. A denomination may be implicated in the inclusive policy under circumstances which do not yet mark it as apostate. Within such an inclusivistic denominational situation, there is need for a distinctly evangelical witness and fellowship. The difficulty of this position likewise is that of locating the transition line to apostasy.

The problem of the inclusivist is that of recognizing an apostasy at all. Once the authority of the scriptural revelation is dissolved, does the term "apostasy" any longer have an objective tone? The question: What is the line? tends easily to become: Who draws the line? among those who abandon the Scriptures as the authoritative criterion.

Is there any substantial reason why the line which ignores the legalism of Greek Orthodoxy (with its denial that salvation is possible except on the condition of baptism) may not ignore also the apostasy of Romanism (with its denial of the sufficiency of Christ's death), or ignore also the heresy of Unitarianism (with its denial of the necessity of Christ's death), or ignore also the paganism of Humanism (with its denial of the validity of supernaturalism in any form)? Perhaps such a line may be maintained by an act of will. But if the line is not grounded in the first place in any final, objective authority, but in an act of will, why may it not be reversed by a contrary act of will at some future date?

III.

Our task is the exhibition of the biblical alternative to the organizational and the separatist views of Christian unity.

The New Testament concept of unity is spiritual. It is misconceived in organizational terms. This can be supported by three considerations. These attest the fact that the unity which the New Testament holds in view involves no external organization to which believers owe a loyalty superior to the local church on the ground that it is the visible articulation of the body of Christ.

A. The apostolic literature assumes that the unity of believers is already a fact of the historical order, not something which remains to be consummated. This is apparent from the Apostle Paul's exhortation to believers "to *preserve* the unity of the Spirit" in the very passage in which the theme of oneness is most conspicuous in his writings (Ephesians 4:3ff.). The indwelling Holy Spirit is the principle of unity in the body of Christ; his pervading presence secures the oneness of believers. "There is one body, and one Spirit." The Body, and its unity, already exists, and does not need to be now produced. This unity may be empirically disturbed by dissension, or empirically promoted by co-operation, but the ultimate unity of the church is neither destroyed by separatism nor established by organizational union. Its unity arises from the fact that there is but one body, one Spirit, one hope, one Lord, one faith, one baptism, one God. These are declarations of fact, not exhortations. All believers, *qua* believers, are in Christ, and constitute but one body (Romans 12:5). The fact of inclusion in or exclusion from any external visible organization is not the touchstone of this unity of which the Apostle speaks, for the unity exists in the spiritual body of which Christ is the head and of which all regenerate believers are members.

B. The disciples for whom Jesus prayed with a view to their future unity were already organizationally one, as members of the apostolic company. Hence the unity toward which the high priestly prayer looks must be spiritual. On the basis of redemption, the disciples were to share in this future spiritual unity through the Spirit's baptism of all believers into one body. After the resurrection the Lord connected both the experience of peace as the bond of their unity, and the ratification of their mission as an extension of the divine vocation of the Redeemer himself, with the gift of the Holy Spirit (John 20:21f.). By the Spirit's operation the lives of his followers are linked in unison with his own life and purpose.

Supportive evidence for this position is not lacking within the high priestly prayer. The twice-spoken petition "that they may be one, even as we are one" (17:11, 22) fixes attention upon a vertical or spiritual relationship, rather than horizontal organization. The Father in heaven and the Son on earth constitute the archetypal unity upon which the unity of the body is predicated. Indubitably the New Testament doctrine of the Trinity predicates a horizontal, or essential, oneness of Father and Son, but the Father-Son unity which supplies the immediate background of the prayer is their spiritual unity despite the spatial separation involved in the Son's humiliation. The model and pattern of the oneness of believers are therefore spiritual, not organizational.

Jesus speaks also of a special glory conferred on his followers with a view to their unity on earth. The words do not have in view that final glory in which both will be united, but a peculiar present glory: "The glory which thou hast given me I have given to them; that they may be one even as we are one." (17:22.) That this glory includes especially the Holy Spirit, who compacts them in one body, is suggested by our next consideration.

C. Our Lord's references to the desired unity among believers compares the relationship to the intimate union of Father and Son: "that they may be one, even as we are one" (17:11), "that they

68

may be one, even as we are one." (17:22.) But the latter verse, which is prefaced by the reference to presently bestowed glory, is followed by a reference to the internal nature of the oneness of believers. Not only does this unity correspond to the oneness of the Father and the Son but, moreover, it is implemented by the Son's indwelling of his followers: *"I in them* and thou in me, that they may become perfectly one."* (17:23.) Thus the unity of believers is constituted by their unique relation to the crucified and risen Christ who indwells his followers. Upon this spiritual relation the unity is predicated. The same emphasis appears in the earlier phrase: "as thou, Father, art in me, and I in thee, that they also may be *in us.*" (17:21.) As the unity of the Father and the Son exists in the intimate reciprocal fellowship which they share, so also the participation of believers in the fellowship of the Father and the Son constitutes their unity.

The New Testament epistles carry forward this emphasis that the Holy Spirit is the agent by whom the *unio mystica* is accomplished. A passage from 1 John—the same John whose Gospel gives us the high priestly prayer—is incontrovertible: "By this we know that we abide in him and he in us, because he has given us of his own Spirit." (4:13.)

These considerations make it necessary to conceive the nature of the unity Christ sustains primarily in a spiritual sense. The oneness of believers is not constituted by ecclesiastical action of any kind, neither by past conclaves in Jerusalem or Rome, nor modern conclaves in Amsterdam or Evanston. The Spirit alone is the author of this unity. The New Testament declares the unity of believers, both that it is a fact and that it must be preserved.

The unity is to be kept, empirically and outwardly, and not alone inwardly. It is to be earnestly and strenuously articulated in the world. The Pauline question: "Is Christ divided?" (1 Corinthians 1:13), addressed to a local church in Corinth, does not lose its force for the Christian conscience universally, any more than does the apostolic exhortation: "I appeal to you, brethren, . . . that there be no divisions among you." (1 Corinthians 1:10.)

How is this empirical unity to be implemented in the mid-twentieth century in which the ecclesiastical simplicity of the apostolic situation has evaporated, and in which church life is encumbered by rigid denominational and antidenominational and super-denominational loyalties?

Not one of the passages bearing on the unity of believers in the New Testament (e.g., 1 Corinthians 1:10, 2 Corinthians 13:11, Romans 14:19, 15:5, Philippians 2:1-3, Colossians 3:12-15) looks in the direction of organizational union for solution. All of them regard the Spirit as the uniting life of the church, the vital principle of cohesion. The New Testament does not define the antithesis of "division" in terms of a single organizational fellowship in which all distinctives blur. The witness of history is that it is the endeavor to implement outward ecclesiastical union which in the long run is provocative of far-reaching schism.

If we look to the early church for a clue as to the way in which its unity was to be preserved, one expression of their fidelity to Christ was that "they devoted themselves to the apostles' teaching and fellowship." (Acts 2:42.) The construction in the original emphasizes their oneness in "the fellowship," i.e., the fellowship which the Lord created by the Spirit, in conjunction with their oneness in the doctrine of the apostles. They were one in faith and doctrine (cf. 1 Timothy 4:6), and they regarded a departure from true doctrine as evidence of a departure from the faith (cf. 1 Timothy 1:21). There is no support in the New Testament for the position that doctrinal liberalism and doctrinal fidelity are to enjoy equal right and dignity within the church of Christ. Both in the statement of postpentecostal unity (Acts 2:42) and of the significance of the inspired Scriptures (2 Timothy 3:16), priority is attached to the importance of revealed truths.

The doctrinal criterion of Christian faith stands before us in the inspired apostolic Scriptures. The early confidence in an authoritative corpus of writings was validated by the Savior (Matthew 5:17f.). The risen Christ had paid peerless tribute to the Old Testament—the law, the writings, the prophets (Luke 24:25, 44). Even the great apostle was careful to enunciate the very heart of the Gospel—the atoning death and bodily resurrection of Christ—in conjunction with the twofold "in accordance with the scriptures." (2 Corinthians 15:3f.) The incarnate Christ had correlated the promise of the Spirit with the assurance of future apostolic teaching. (John 14:26, 16:13f.) The early church prided itself not on how little it needed to believe as a basis of fellowship, but on how much it dared believe in view of an assured revelation.

The unity Christ sustains is a spiritual unity. Its life is the share in the same love which the Father has for the Son, which regen-

70

erate believers enjoy in consequence of their redemption. Its identity is preserved by the indwelling of the Holy Spirit, constituting all regenerate believers a single body responsive to the lordship of Christ. The true church is not an organization merely; it is an organism, a biological, a spiritual reality. This body recognizes no God but the God and Father of our Lord Jesus Christ. It recognizes no Jesus but the virgin-born, sinless, divine, mediating, resurrected, and returning Lord. It recognizes no Spirit but the Spirit who has articulated the Word of God in Scripture as the only authoritative Christian rule of faith and practice.

The believing church, therefore, is hesitant to project a public expression of its unity which compromises any of these realities. It has little enthusiasm for a theological index which—even if it avoids a full concession to the view that doctrinal distinctions are of no ultimate significance—nevertheless is ambiguous enough to admit of both a biblical and nonbiblical meaning, and thus to give Christian unity the character of an inclusive rather than of an exclusive fellowship.

But, it may be asked, How is this bare emphasis on spiritual unity to be translated practically into the concrete historical setting of our generation? How is principle to be moved into the modern scene in terms of workable suggestions? What attitude does it imply toward the present merger of denominations, in view of the growing recognition that such distinctions are not ultimate? What public and external expression of spiritual unity is legitimate?

While a comprehensive answer to these questions must be forged by the evangelical conscience at large, in the course of obedience to the risen Lord and his revealed will, some observations are almost self-evident. If Christian unity includes doctrinal harmony, the expanded inclusivism of amalgamating groups already committed to an inclusivistic base may constitute a more fundamental witness to doctrinal indifference than to essential spiritual unity and may enforce the fallacious idea that genuine Christian unity is proportioned to numerical largeness and theological inclusivism. On the other hand, the deliberate cultivation of independency, as a reaction to the fear of doctrinal inclusivism, is an equally unacceptable exposition of Christian unity. There can be no sound evangelical hostility to denominational mergers which involve no sacrifice of a biblical doctrinal basis, but rather preserve this.

Nevertheless, these outward amalgamations neither create nor maintain the essential unity of the body. Organizational union

71

may exist where spiritual disunion prevails, and spiritual union may prevail in the absence of organizational union. The one indispensable New Testament factor is spiritual unity. Where this exists, other partitions and unities will sooner or later fall away under their own weight.

Evangelical Christianity sets out self-consciously from the written Word and the inner witness of the Spirit to attract voluntary cooperation in an efficient and effective outer witness to the world, and in the articulation of the mutual concerns of co-operating believers. Evangelical unity is voluntary in spirit, rather than coercive in temper. It involves no claim to be the divinely appointed voice of the whole body of Christ. Nor does it disdain genuine believers who are "not of us" as though they are any less members of the body, thus implying some criterion of "acceptability" superior to the lordship of Christ in the believer's life, and thus regarding him as divisive simply on account of his nonparticipation. Presuming to speak only for those who have voluntarily identified themselves, evangelical Christianity nonetheless seeks through its corporate effort to advance the concerns of the whole body, and grieves over whatever frustrates anywhere an effective witness by regenerate believers.

The body of Christ is already empirically manifested in visible churches created by the Spirit of God in the midst of the fallen world. The historical manifestation of the body must always be incomplete prior to the Lord's return, not only because of the remnants of sin in the community of faith, but because of its chronological limitations in history, and the essentially spiritual rather than organizational unity of the body. No biblical warrant exists for one visible historical church or organization, be it Protestant or Roman Catholic, regarded as the superlative manifestation of the body of Christ. The body of Christ on earth has one consuming passion: that the Spirit, through the widest and fullest preaching of the Gospel, may regenerate souls, rescuing them from their lost condition. The members of this body yearn for the fellowship and spiritual unity of distinct churches which are true in faith and doctrine. And in so doing, they manifest their continuity with the Christian community of apostolic times.

Chapter Six

The Church Unity We Have
Albert C. Outler

Professor of Theology, Perkins School of Theology; Methodist Church

It is important to keep clear the crucial distinction between the *nature* of the unity we seek and the *mode* which that unity may take. There are those who fear the ecumenical movement because they suppose it is already committed to a predetermined mode of unity. They think it is to be a super-church, a collective of Christians in lock step, a totalitarian community opposed not only to division but to diversity as well. On the other hand, there are those who are impatient with the movement because it has not come up with a comprehensive and detailed program, has not even produced a "working model" of the "coming great church."

Both groups—the fearful and the impatient—need to be reminded that the leaders of the ecumenical movement, at every level, have been consistently urgent and patient at one and the same time. There is wide and deep consensus as to the goal before us: unity in Christ, as fully and as quickly as possible. But the ecumenical movement has conscientiously avoided any precise prescription for this unity. For careful evidence on this score everyone should read the important article by W. A. Visser 't Hooft, "Various Meanings of Unity and the Unity Which the World Council of Churches Seeks to Promote," in the *Ecumenical Review* for October, 1955.

Ecumenical Christians are a company on pilgrimage toward a promised land—but we have no map of the road to it. Already the Holy Spirit has led us past obstacles and impasses that seemed insuperable. We have moved farther in the last fifty years than in the previous thousand. The Spirit is still our chief reliance in the onward journey. We are sure of our goal, but we must resist the temptation to predetermine the route. This willingness—partial, to be sure—to trust the Spirit's leading forms part of the peculiar genius of the modern ecumenical movement. It had best not be lost if we are still to go forward, together.

Christianity has always been plagued by divisions. Christians have always been seeking and hoping for unity. No Christian can ever fully accept factions and disunity as right among Christians. But serious trouble comes between divided Christians when their mutual concern for unity is expressed in dogmatic formulas to which the dissident parties must agree as conditions of reconciliation. Such attempts at reunion have regularly failed. Their history makes heart-rending reading, but it points a moral which the modern ecumenical movement has learned, at least in part. One of the basic differences between this and earlier ecumenical efforts is the present stress on mutual recognition between Christians of their fellowship as Christians, here and now, in advance of full doctrinal consensus.

The modern ecumenical movement has made it possible—and, in a sense, has made it necessary—for divided Christians to begin with the recognition of the unity we actually have, and thus to acknowledge the Christian *koinōnia* that exists even now in and among the divided churches. To share in the ecumenical enterprise, no church is required to renounce its claims as a Christian fellowship, although every church is invited to self-examination and repentance. No church is required to bow to the claims of any other, although all the churches may receive the contributions of all the rest in a fuller richness than any now possesses. Any church may claim for itself the plenary fullness of the Christian tradition, and may decline to recognize certain other churches as fully valid and authentic. But no church may refuse to acknowledge a *vestigium ecclesiae,* a "vestige of the church," in any other church which seriously and sincerely confesses Jesus Christ as God and Savior.

In this way, the modern ecumenical movement has renewed the Christian sense of community without imposing a specific and predetermined pattern upon it. Ecumenical Christians begin by recognizing each other as somehow included in the household of God, by the seal and the power of the Holy Spirit. Within this fellowship, we are enabled, even compelled, to discuss the great issues which currently inhibit our fuller and more valid unity in faith and order, life and work.

This initial mutual recognition of our unity in Christ is not enough in itself. The unity we seek is one which will overcome and transform the present clefts and inequities within the visible churches. It is a unity without defenses and condescensions. But this fuller unity—to which the Holy Spirit will lead us as fast as we are willing to be led—can be more surely achieved within a community of churches that recognize each other than between a congeries of churches demanding detailed consensus as the precondition of recognition and the ecumenical endeavor.

Does this mean that the unity we seek is only an ideal vision— some far-off divine event toward which the ecumenical movement yearns? Does it mean that fullness of the church does not now exist but might be achieved by amiable Christians who would agree to ignore or minimize the quarrelsome issues between them? Some of our Roman Catholic friends suspect us of espousing just such an Erasmian view of ecumenicity. In a very significant survey of recent developments (*Histoire doctrinale du mouvement œcuménique*) Canon Gustave Thils argues that the World Council of Churches regards true unity as only a future prospect, not as a present reality. He writes:

> It seems fair to say, that the majority of the Christian groups who make up the World Council of Churches maintain a conception of the church according to which: (a) the true church of Christ does not now exist in its real essence *(quoad substantiam)* in any historical communion; and (b) since this is the case and since the essential unity of this visible historical church does not actually exist at the present time, the divided churches must proceed to *become the Una Sancta,* through the gift of God and by means of their unanimous action.

If this were the mind of the ecumenical movement, our quest for unity would be foredoomed. For this would imply that full and authentic salvation is impossible within any presently existing church among the separated churches—unless there is one of them which is and always has been the *Una Sancta.* A Christian church might admit that, as it is presently constituted and related to the other churches, it cannot be fully identified as the *Una Sancta.* But no church doubts that the essential unity of the Body of Christ is real and present within its communal life, even though this unity is not now fully manifest. Nor can it deny the reality of the *Una Sancta* in other churches who confess the same Lord, who are sealed by the same Spirit in baptism, who cherish the same *koinōnia* in Christ Jesus. It is this mutual acknowledgment of the present reality of the *Una Sancta* which is the essential bond and motive power of the ecumenical movement.

The unity we seek is the fulfillment of the unity we have. For we have already discovered among us a unity far deeper than our differences. Already we are aware that the Holy Spirit is among us, manifesting to us our common Lord. This unity we have is a gift which we have been given—in God's great proffer of grace and truth in Jesus Christ. It is a unity which generates community even in advance of doctrinal elaboration and consensus. The community thus created is obliged to seek honest understanding and agreement in matters of faith and order, in the temper and by methods consonant with the basic reality of this Christian community. For community in faith is more basic than consensus in doctrine.

The unity we seek includes the hope and expectation of a universal ministry and valid sacramental communion; but it demands neither of these as preconditions of continued search for an adequate basis for them. The unity we seek frankly includes the ideal of diversity in unity and allows for flexible and adaptable patterns in polity, liturgy and theology. But the unity we seek is not a unity that is an end in itself. The real justification for unity is that it may enable us to obey Christ's great commission of world-wide evangelism: "that the world may believe . . . that the world may know . . ." (John 17:21, 23).

This basic conception of the unity we seek appears in *The Evanston Report*—a statement which reflects a basic ecumenical perspective:

> From the beginning the Church has been given an indissoluble unity in Christ, by reason of His self-identification with His people. But the Church has never realized the fullness of that unity. . . . Thus we may speak of the oneness of the Church in its earthly pilgrimage as a growth from its unity, as given, to its unity, as fully manifested (*Eph.* 4:3, 13). . . . It would be ungrateful to a merciful God if we did not speak now of these gifts which assure us that the undivided Christ is present amongst us, pouring His life into us all, in spite of our divisions. . . . As we have come to know each other better in the World Council of Churches, we have come to appreciate the immense range of common practice and intention which we share. . . . We give thanks to our Father for these evidences that our

unity in Christ is a present reality, both in the World Council of Churches and in relation to other Christians whose fellowship we do not as yet fully enjoy [pp. 84, 86].

The community thus far achieved in the ecumenical movement is very far from a community in full Christian accord. And yet the experience of Christian fellowship we have already had has created an atmosphere in which we may go on seeking a fuller unity and a temper which prompts us to be discontent with anything less than the fullness of the earnest we have already received. If we had begun by adopting some sort of prescription for unity and trying to impose this upon divided Christians, we would still be haggling over doctrinal differences—or, what is much more likely, we would long since have lost the will to remain together. As it is—and providentially, I believe—the fellowship we have experienced has enabled us to recognize the unity we have and to cherish the possibility of its fuller realization. Thus the way has been opened for continuing common search, for new achievement in ecumenical theologizing and for new expectations of unpredictable progress.

This unity we have comes from our common reception of *the* Christian tradition. There is, and always has been, a singular Christian tradition which transcends and measures all the plural traditions of the churches, which stands at the center of the Scriptures themselves. It is to this tradition that the Scriptures point and to which all derivative traditions must appeal. It constitutes the authority of the church and defines the nature (though not necessarily the mode) of Christian unity. All Christians in every age have had some real awareness of this pre-eminent tradition and its fundamental authority for faith and order.

The Christian tradition, in its essential form, is God's redemptive act in "handing over" and "handing down" (*paradidonai, tradere*) Jesus Christ to share our human lot and to reconcile the world to himself (cf. Rom. 8:31-32; 4:24-25; Gal. 2:20; Eph. 5:2, 25; cf. also 1 Cor. 15:24 for the eschatological "tradition" "when Christ delivers [*paradido*] the kingdom of God the Father after destroying every other rule and every authority and power"). This tradition was God's deed, God's Word, to which the apostles and the church were called as witnesses, stewards and proclaimers (Acts 1:8). What they received from God, they were commissioned "to hand over" to others. The Christian tradition is Jesus

77

Christ: witnessed and proclaimed by the power of the Holy Spirit; confessed as Lord and Savior to the glory of God the Father; heard and obeyed as the Word of God, the Head of the church, in which faithful men are truly members one of another. The authority of the New Testament derives from its definitive witness to this tradition of the Word of God, and its power to transmit this Word to men in undiminished power and relevance. The authority of Christian preaching depends upon its faithfulness in representing this tradition in all its fullness and truth. Thus St. Paul could appeal to this tradition as the warrant for his apostolate and his unity with the other apostles: "For I received of the Lord what I then 'handed over' (*paredoka*) to you, that on the night in which he was 'handed over' (*paredidete*) [to death] the Lord Jesus took bread," etc. (1 Cor. 11:23; see also 15:3-11, for the tradition of the resurrection-kērygma).

The true unity of Christians is their reception of God's gift in Christ and their acceptance of Christ's commission to share the gospel with every creature (see the vivid passages in Ignatius, *Philadelphians* 5, 8, 9, in which the martyr-bishop confesses Jesus Christ as *the* Christian tradition). Men cannot know this unity or express its import for living save by the witness and illumination of the Holy Spirit. Yet once the pentecostal faith is kindled, the way is opened to search for appropriate ways of thought and worship to celebrate God's grace in worship and doctrine. And when this search for appropriate interpretation and celebration goes awry, when Christians contend against each other in worship of the one Lord Christ, when plural and antagonistic traditions arise, the only hope for restored unity lies in a return to the primordial tradition and the primordial imperatives of the gospel. The revelation of God in Christ and the commissioning of the church by Christ through the Paraclete is *the* Christian tradition. It is the sole referent of the apostolic preaching, the authentic form of Scripture, the valid authority of the fathers and the councils. The common intent of any Christian group is to receive God's gifts in Christ, to have the Spirit renew it in faithful hearts, to transmit it faithfully and effectively, from generation to generation, "to all nations" (Matt. 28:19).

It would take more than a short article to show the practical bearing of this conception of the Christian tradition on the harsh and knotty problems of the separated churches. And yet we cannot even begin to face these problems seriously unless we do so in a sincere sense of *present* unity. What we are seeking is not a unity that we have never known at all; rather, we yearn for the fulfillment of the unity we know already, but do not know well enough. In the ecumenical movement our hopes rise and fall as we meet successes and setbacks. But more important than our achievements is the foundation on which they rest. The foundation of our ecumenical work is not *our* achievement; it has already been laid for us by God and we are building upon it even now, in one way or another yet to be judged (1 Cor. 3:10-15).

Two constant dangers must be avoided at all costs. One is the premature demand for a showdown, a crisis which confronts men with the false choice of unity at the price of treason to a treasured heritage. We know what their choice will be—and rightly, unless they can be persuaded that the unity we are seeking together will also conserve the authentic treasures which each tradition has to bring to the common life in the body of Christ.

The other danger is the premature delineation of a blueprint of the reunited church. Divided Christians must not be asked to foresee the detailed shape of things to come, for our present prejudices are bound to distort the clarity and scope of our vision. Does one of the existing churches exhibit the true pattern to which the rest of us must come eventually? If this be so, many of us cannot recognize it at the present moment, and it is useless to deplore our myopia. Will a new and quite unpredictable form of Christian unity emerge which can include and conserve the vital goods in every present tradition? Many of us devoutly believe that this is the better prospect, but would not presume to spell it out at this time.

The genius and the promise of the modern ecumenical movement is that none of us has to foreknow the future in order to move toward it confidently. It suffices to recognize the unity we have already, to remember the unexpected turns of the ecumenical enterprise in its progress through the last half-century, and to keep clear and steady the right goal: oneness in Christ, "that the world may believe."

Those who have experienced the "ecumenical fact," who have known the frustrations and sudden exaltations of ecumenical work, who have come to expect the unexpected in the unfolding life of the movement—all these can testify to the dynamic and transforming effect of this great work of grace in our time. We can claim, in all humility, already to understand something of the living wonder of the *Una Sancta*. It may very well be that there are those among us who understand it more fully than the rest of us. But even they have no higher authority than that which all of us must learn to acknowledge: the tradition of the Incarnate Word, whom none of us may rightly ignore or reject. And we shall come more quickly and more surely to the full unity of the faith if we continue in the unity we have received and have recognized in each other. In this disposition and commitment we may continue our search for pure doctrines, for valid polities, for adequate liturgies— all under the authority and judgment of the regnant Spirit, sent of the Father to lead us into the freedom of the truth.

As long as something like this continues to be the temper of our fellowship, we can be certain that the ecumenical movement is God's doing, wondrous in our sight, in which he is bringing to fruition, past our wisdom and our obstinacy, the full and true unity which he wills, and for which we work and pray.

Chapter Seven

A Southern Baptist
Views Church Unity

Theron D. Price

Professor of Church History, Southern Baptist Theological Seminary, Louisville; Southern Baptist Convention

I.

All truly spiritual treasures require appropriation. Our existence as Christians derives from Christ's gift of himself—for us, in
us, with us. Yet the whole Christian life may be called a quest
for and in Christ; that is, his grace, which is our sure possession,
requires response, appropriation and stewardship. The unity of
the Church in Christ is also such a spiritual treasure. In Christ this
unity is given. Anything too weak to subvert the work of Christ
is too weak to destroy this unity which his work creates and bestows. Yet the whole life of the Church in the world may be
called a quest for and in unity. His gift of our oneness with
himself, and with one another in him, requires response, appropriation and stewardship.

The unity we seek is, therefore, a unity we have; and to reject
the quest is to reject Christ for the spirit of faction. This appears to be essentially what 1 Corinthians is about. This unity in
Christ and the Church is an actual state of oneness. Viewed as
the gift or work of Christ, it pertains to what is by nature simple.
Viewed as the result of his work, it pertains to an indissoluble involvement of parts in a complex whole. The substantive "unity,"
used in the Christian sense, refers to something we have and become, rather than to something which we have not and produce;
i.e., the substantive belongs with the intransitive rather than the
transitive verb "to unite."

Stig Hanson has shown[1] that we encounter in the New Testament not only a consciousness of unity which lies at the basis of biblical thought, and is a condition of it; but, also, a conscious reflection upon the religious idea of unity itself.

Our natures seem to require the displacement of chaos by the realization of unity and continuity in the orders of existence. In this sense unity is primarily an instinct or drive. This displacement, for serious and perceptive souls, is the result of conquest through struggle. Apart from such instinct and struggle there would be, for us, no conquest of chaos, and therefore no cosmos and no culture.

While these aspects of unity are important, one needs to be reminded that instinct and struggle do not cover all the question. The believer sees God as the ground and goal of our unity.[2] For, to the believer, unity is essentially reconciliation across a gulf of alienation. It rests on divine initiative. It is revealed, effected, and consummated in Jesus Christ. It has both historical and eschatological dimensions: i.e., it both is, and is to be.

This unity with God in Christ, by means of the Holy Spirit, is deployed in variety through the members of Christ, his body the Church. There is but one body and one Spirit, even as there is but one Lord and one faith (Ephesians 4:4-6). Unity in this biblical sense rests on the grace of the triune, sovereign God; that is to say, here is unity as gift. As the real gift of the real God, it is real unity. It cannot be understood or realized apart from him who bestows it in Christ by the Spirit. Christ *is* the unity of his Church. As there is but one Lord, one faith, and one baptism, there can be only one Church; and the actual existence of the one Church of Jesus Christ is part of the fundamental Christian confession. The creeds and platforms of Christendom are at one on this.

All this entails two affirmations which, one may believe, are of basic importance to the question of and the quest for unity. First, where Christ is present and known to faith, there is the Church; second, concern for the unity of the Church is concern for Christ.

---

[1]Hanson, S., *The Unity of the Church in the New Testament (Acta Seminarii Neotestamentici Upsaliensis,* XIV), Uppsala, 1946, pp. 1-4. The reflection on unity is especially to the fore in Ephesians, Colossians, and John.

[2]This never means that "God" is the designation we give to a ground of unity which we are able of ourselves to discern or to effect. The word "God" rather designates a Person than describes a class. The word pertains not to an idea on which we may choose to reflect; it confronts us with the Being with whom we have to do, whether we reflect thereon or no, and in whom we co-exist.

"Where Christ is present and known to faith, there is the Church." As P. T. Forsyth reminds us,[3] to be in Christ is to be in Christ's society, the Church. The Church is precisely those who are with Christ, who worship and serve him as Lord. The sphere in all the universe in which Christ could never require a vicar or proxy is the Church. Here he is present himself and is known to faith. This not only eliminates the principle of Papacy from the doctrine of the Church; it also eliminates episcopacy as belonging to the *esse* of the Church. The real and efficacious presence of the living Christ also eliminates any kind of sacerdotalism from the Church. The only priesthood in the Church is the derivative priesthood of the whole people of God, in their relation to the Great High Priest. The only essential ministry in the Church is the ministry of Christ himself.

"Concern for the unity of the Church is concern for Christ." Concern for the *Una Sancta* is Christian concern only as it is concern for Christ, for his worship and service. Conversely, to be concerned for the presence, worship, and service of Christ is to be concerned for the only true unity of the Church. Christ is not divided, and those who are one in him are not divided.

The unity of the Church comes to expression in preaching, Baptism, Supper. But we must never forget that it is the Word of God in *Christ* that is preached. Also, Baptism is essentially a free and gracious act of God in *Christ* of which immersion in water is an accompanying sign, seal, and symbol. The Lord's Supper is indeed the *Lord's Supper,* a participation in *Christ's* body and blood of which the loaf and the cup are sign, seal, and symbol (1 Corinthians 10:16-17). All three, preaching, Baptism, Supper, address themselves to faith as the only true correlative of divine action. Where God speaks and acts man can only believe and obey, or else disbelieve and disobey. God, being really God, is the ground of the world's unity even as he is the source of its life. The Church is the People who by faith know that this is so, and who submit to the God whom they personally encounter as Person in Jesus Christ. Without such obedient faith (understood as divinely bestowed and evoked response to his own pres-

---

[3]Forsyth, P. T., *The Church and the Sacraments,* London, 1953, pp. 61f. Essentially the same theme was elaborated in 1936 by Karl Barth, in his message to the approaching Faith and Order meeting at Edinburgh, 1937; and it is stated once more by Anders Nygren, *Christ and His Church,* Philadelphia, 1956, pp. 89-107. Here Congregationalist, Reformed, and Lutheran speak agreeably with our early Baptist confessions of faith. Cf. W. J. McGlothlin, *Baptist Confessions of Faith,* Philadelphia, 1911, *passim.*

ence in Christ by the Spirit), there is no Church, no Baptism, no Supper. No amount of doctrinal correctness or right order can make any ecclesiastical society to be the Church. The Church is in and with Christ.

But the Church is also *under* Christ, and, so long as it is truly Church, is always under Christ. The Church is called into being by the gospel of Christ. It stands under the judgment and grace of what produces it. Perhaps, indeed, the Church is never so truly the Church as when acknowledging its dependent status in grace, and confessing its sin and need. Certainly, a claim to infallibility of teaching or to irreformability of institutions is an indication more of pride than of grace, and rests upon promises which were never made by the Christ in whom the Church consists.

The Church is represented in the New Testament as the congregation of believers—and these who believe are those who both are incorporated into Christ and share the fellowship of the Spirit. At the same time, the Church is the body of Christ—and this body of Christ is the congregation of believers who share the fellowship of the Spirit. The Church is the fellowship of the Spirit—and this fellowship of the Spirit is the congregation of those who both believe in Christ and are incorporated into him. Confession, incorporation, and experience are thus necessary to make into Church what would otherwise be merely an association of men.[4]

II

Baptists rightly understand the relation of the Church to the churches to be rooted in and contingent upon the unity of the Church in Christ. Though our own doctrine at this point is as often misunderstood by our own people as by others, our real contention is that we would lay no other foundation for unity than that which is already laid in the Lord of the Church.

The Baptists have maintained from conviction what is, in its distinctive form, a minority viewpoint on the nature of a local church. The development of our language (under the stimulus of ideas which are not too fortunate) makes it more or less necessary to speak of various denominations of Christians as "Churches." From our theological viewpoint, this appears as a

[4]The form of this paragraph is obviously influenced by Lesslie Newbigin's excellent book, *The Household of God*, New York, 1954. This book is replete with the Scripture references which support this threefold argument on the nature of the Church.

misuse of words. There is, in the strictest sense, no Methodist *Church* or Presbyterian *Church* or Baptist *Church*. In the measure that such an entity took itself seriously as Church, it would involve considering other such entities as false Churches. Most evangelical Christians agree that such a body would be a misguided sect.[5] The Church is one, not many. A denomination is a group of Christians of similar enough doctrine and order to cohere in the expression thereof. Churches are related in various ways to form a denomination. But denominations are never related in such a way as to compose the Church. That is, denominational titles are always and only designations for identifiable groups of people who profess to belong to the Church.

The Baptist view of the local church is that it is, in its place and time, an embodiment and manifestation of the Church of Jesus Christ. The Church is truly known only to faith, because it is constituted in and by the Holy Spirit. In this sense only can the Church be happily described as invisible; for the Church becomes visible in churches or congregations. In whatever congregation Christ is actually present and effecting his will through Word and Worship, there is a church. For here, in such a congregation, faith in Christ is confessed; here believers adore him and are fitted as members into the common life of his body; here the fellowship of the Holy Spirit is an experienced miracle.

There will be weak faith, moral frailty, and self-centered individualism in all of the people in varying degrees. But, as is true of the Church itself, such a fallible congregation with the presence of Christ in it derives its fundamental character not from its members but from its Head. Such a congregation must seek to accept as its members only those, and all of those, whom Christ himself has received through faith in him.

It is not the purpose of this article to treat the problem of the sense and measure in which denominations whose membership is determined on principles other than these, represent and embody

---

[5]We leave out of consideration the Roman Catholic denomination of Christians, which, by its own official definition, must appear to evangelical understanding as a sect. It could be added here that, although until about one hundred years ago it was not uncommon for Baptists in America to speak of "the Baptist Church," they understood the phrase to mean the denomination of Baptists. Though the phrase is no longer used, it is unhappily true that some Southern Baptists—while rejecting the term "Church" as the right designation for our convention of Christians—actually do consider our churches to be the only true churches, or, as the case may be, the only true representatives of the Church. This is, from the viewpoint of the New Testament, to act as a sect. How this expresses itself within our own immediate family, is seen in the manner in which some Southern Baptists think of our Convention as a denomination. Thus American (Northern) Baptists appear to this group as a separate denomination of Christians, rather than as another convention of the same denomination. This is sectarianism in the guise of civil war. In this we need to repent.

the Church. Any convinced Baptist would say, however, that in the measure that the principle of faith is applied to the Church, in that measure the parish principle, and the baptism of infants on which it rests, are called into question. A high churchmanship, properly so called—a churchmanship which takes seriously and simultaneously both the Church and the churches—will ever be seeking for the local church all and only of what pertains to the Church of Christ. And the Church has not to speak of a Christ who is yet to be received by faith, nor of a grace which is merely pledged in sovereign freedom. A local church—in whatever measure it is Church—is a group of people who *have* received Jesus Christ by faith; who have received, through this faith, the grace which in his sovereign freedom he bestows. And one who does not so believe in Christ, and participate personally in his grace, should not be in a church because he is not in the Church.

The Baptist principle involves a high doctrine of the local congregation because of its understanding of the primacy of the Church Universal. For in every congregation, rightly called and ordered, there is the fullness of churchmanship. God in Christ by the Spirit is present in every congregation. Each congregation thus encounters the living Reality and Truth. Beyond this nothing is referable, and nothing else is more ultimate. No one congregation has more of God's interest than another, nor does any have more direct access to his presence and power. Hence, no church or group of churches may coerce the will of another. Each congregation is independent; but it is always the participation of each church in the life of the Whole Church which gives each church its authority and relevance. At the same time, the churches are interdependent; and this requires to be expressed in association and co-operation. We have a common faith in God, a common life in Christ, a common experience in the Holy Spirit.

This all settles down to the question of the actual relations of various groups of Christian people.

III

The foregoing exposition represents the major tradition of Baptist faith and practice. It is a backdrop against which present Southern Baptist attitudes may be understood. It is the difficult task of this concluding section to interpret my brethren in relation to the question of unity.

Two things may first be said: one, the generalizations which follow certainly do not, in a single instance, represent the mind of all Southern Baptists; and two, there will be many of my brethren who would not subscribe even to my highly generalized interpretation. We have great numbers of pastors who, for example, subscribe to the view of the Church already expounded. But we also have many who would dissent from the essential doctrine itself, and many more who would formulate the question differently.

Southern Baptist churches represent a majority movement in the regions to which they belong. We tend—partly because we are busy with the work which we believe God has given us to do—to be oblivious to the need for wider unity. This is in no sense to suggest that our churches are ordinarily "unneighborly." There is often, in many cities especially, a co-operation with other denominations at the local level. But because our patterns of thought are markedly regional in character, we tend to see no need for co-operation beyond the local level. We are not today as aware as were our forebears that the doctrine of the Church and the unity of the Church are inseparably intertwined.

In what measure any group of Christians disbelieve in the mystical body which is constituted by the one Spirit, in that measure they sin against their own life. But it would be difficult to convince us that the visible reduction of the mystical body to one legal corporation would enhance the true unity of the Church. In whatever measure this is even a subsidiary aim of the leadership of the World Council of Churches, it will be met with a stubborn resistance by Southern Baptists. Most of us would probably feel that we can do no more for a divided Christendom (though this is not a divided Church) than to try to understand ourselves and interpret ourselves in love to our fellow believers.[6]

Whenever Christians refuse the inconvenience of this understanding and communication, or are divided from one another by unchristian tempers and suspicious attitudes, it is a sin which nothing can excuse. But this is not identical with saying that it is sinful for some Christians to be Episcopalians, while others are Methodists, Baptists, or Presbyterians.[7] Our ecclesiastical divisions *per se* are less serious than lukewarm faith and feeble love.

---

[6]Charles Gore, *mutatis mutandis,* would apparently have felt at one with us in this score. Cf. G. L. Prestige, *The Life of Charles Gore,* London, 1935, pp. 378, 450, 454, 503.
[7]Denney, James, *The Church and the Kingdom,* London, n.d. pp. 145 f.

We must come to love each other as Christ loved us. In such a context we can converse with our guards down and our hearts open. In the common submission of our minds to the Word and Spirit of God we can learn from each other, we can gain larger agreements through fellowship, and, where necessary, we can agree in love to disagree. It is the writer's feeling that we Southern Baptists are in much greater danger, at present, of failing to make our witness to the Whole Church by isolation than of losing the distinctiveness of that witness by association.

With specific reference to our participation in the World Council of Churches: It is obvious that there is nothing distinctively Baptistic to prevent it. Numerous other Baptist Conventions or Unions are able to co-operate on terms which threaten neither our doctrine nor our polity. We could, on principle, co-operate—in such way as to jeopardize none of our principles, and without construing our Convention as a Church. But for various reasons and convictions, as well as prejudices and fears, we have refrained, and probably will continue to refrain from participation.

John Henry Newman somewhere says: "When men understand each other's meaning, they see, for the most part, that controversy is either superfluous or hopeless." We need to understand one another better as we come closer to one another in God. In our finite and sinful situation we shall discover issues on which agreement seems hopeless; but as we draw nearer to one another in the love of God we shall doubtless discover that some of our controversies are superfluous. John Mackay's recent words find echo in the writer's soul:

> Let us reject forever the thought that the unity of Christ's Church Universal must ever be based upon a lowest common denominator formula. Far from that. Let Christian churchmen in full loyalty to Christ, to the biblical revelation and to the Church Universal seek, in an agony of prayer, in self-criticism and in adventurous faith, to bring what is authentically Christian into the treasure chamber of the Church which is Christ's Body.[8]

---

[8]Mackay, J. A., "John Baillie, a Lyrical Tribute and Appraisal," in *Scottish Journal of Theology*, Vol. 9, No. 3 (Sept., 1956), p. 235.

Chapter Eight

A Historic Free Church View

John Yoder

Director of Relief Activities of the Mennonite Central
Committee; Mennonite Church

That the unity we seek should be an expression of the unity
we have has become a commonplace in recent ecumenical thinking. But the assent to the proposition that Christian unity is a
given reality, and not something to be created, has not yet modi-
fied the shape of efforts toward a visible expression of that given
fact in church order and church life. The discussion of Christian
unity in the past has leapt to two questions: "Do we want federation, fusion, or intercommunion?" and "What shall we do together?" with a rapidity which assumed that all the basic questions were settled. To what extent this short circuit has truly
furthered the cause, it is not up to us to decide; but we can ask at
least that henceforth the relation between schemes of union and
the givenness of unity be kept clearer.

I. The Unity We Seek Is Conversation

If I admit the givenness of unity between my interlocutor, whose
good faith in confessing the Name of Christ I have no grounds to
question, and myself, I thereby lay upon myself, as upon him, the
imperative of conversation at those points where, in life and doctrine, our given unity is hidden by disagreement. I am released
from this obligation only when we have come to agreement, or
when my interlocutor refuses further to converse.

Superficially, the ecumenical discussions of the past half century
have produced one good effect. Christian bodies have become
acquainted with one another, have learned to appreciate the sincerity with which strongly variant positions may be held, and

have sought to see the good in others' points of view. Yet, as has been learned in recent years, that is not conversation. It is information, and indispensable as such; but it is in itself not conversation because it does not lead toward agreement, but in fact to crystallizing fundamental differences. True conversation exists only where there is movement toward agreement, motivated by appeal to an authority recognized by both parties. If there is not such movement, talking about the differences only serves to harden them.

The formal requirement for conversation is thus two-sided. (1) Objectively, there must be a mutually recognized authority to which both parties have recourse for ultimate proof, just as physicists have an objective point of reference in their measurements of mass and movement, and historians in their documentary sources; and (2) subjectively, there must be the willingness to move, to change positions, when the proof has been brought. When we say that Christian unity is given, that means that the objective requirement has been met, whether we accept it or not.

The tact with which ecumenical conversation has hitherto gone about the process of getting acquainted without asking anyone to move, and the peculiar character of American denominationalism, in which many organizational divisions do not correspond to any real differences of principle, have obscured the cruciality of *the problem of authority* with which true conversation must begin. It has not been asked clearly wherein that common authority resides before which every party to the conversation was willing to be judged.

For Roman Catholicism the solution is the easiest. The court of appeal is an institution, available in history, with an authorized spokesman. The objective requirement, that there be a definable point of reference, is met admirably. No one can disagree (except with regard to a few awkward moments in the Middle Ages) about who is Pope. At the same time the subjective requirement for conversation is rendered unattainable by definition. Since the Roman Catholic Church is its own final authority, it is inconceivable, at least in principle, that it converse with anyone.

What is less generally recognized is that, speaking formally, American liberal and post-liberal Protestantism is little different from Rome. Like Rome, it presupposes as undebatable a centuries-long doctrinal and institutional evolution which is not open to question from outside itself. The only difference is that this evolution has gone down another track for four or five centuries. Instead of the Counter-reformation, Papal Infallibility, and the Assumption of Mary, its dogma is drawn from the Renaissance, the Reformation, the Enlightenment, Idealism, the scientific world view, and (most recent acquisition) a revived Judeo-Christian doctrine of Sin. In the institutional realm, Greco-Roman ideals of equity and due process of law and Occidental ideals of democracy are not subject to criticism. Built as it is on layer upon layer of ideological affluvium which it dares not submit to too close a scrutiny, this theological position is just as incapable of talking across the fence as is Rome. The only formal difference is that it is more difficult to identify its Pope; but the consensus of what the most popular teachers in the largest seminaries were teaching twenty years ago serves the same purpose. The affirmations of the Bible and of classical orthodoxy can be accepted by American liberal Protestantism only if redefined into terms of psychology and social ethics which are meaningful to modern man. The recent rehabilitation of a doctrine of Sin by certain segments of this thought-world comes neither from the Bible nor from classical orthodoxy, but from the observation by modern man of how much trouble he has getting along with himself.

The rest of Christendom generally differs from Rome and from liberalism simply by choosing some other point along the time scale of doctrinal and institutional evolution to which to tie their ability to converse. Anglo-Catholicism and Eastern Orthodoxy would part with Rome at varying dates, depending upon how much catholicity they want to conserve. Reformation Protestantism chose to revert to the level about A.D. 500, thus avoiding Popery and the Mass but maintaining the State Church, the accepted doctrinal formulations concerning the Trinity and the Natures of Christ, and the persecution of heretics. The Nestorians would back up a little farther yet, and so on and on. . . .

If the locus of our given unity is Jesus Christ, it would seem that the only feasible solution to the problem of authority would be to declare inadmissible the attribution of authoritative character to any particular historical development and to recognize, as the only legitimate Judge, *Christ himself* as he is made known through Scripture to the congregation of those who seek to know him and his will. This would not necessarily mean that all evolution would *ipso facto* be condemned, nor would it commit us to an infantile literalism in the use of Scripture; but there would have to be the mutual abandon of any attempt to have recourse to any particular evolution as a canon of interpretation. Neither what modern man can accept, nor what medieval man could accept, nor what one of the Councils of Constantinople could accept, would have the right to stand above, or beside, or even authoritatively under Christ and Scripture.

This is the position held by the Free Church tradition; by the Swiss and Hutterian Brethren and the Doopsgezinde of the sixteenth century, by the Congregationalists, Baptists, and Quakers later in England, by most of the churches born and reared on the American frontier in the eighteenth and nineteenth centuries. It has spoken less than its share in ecumenical discussion in recent years. This is partly because its lack of interest in doctrinal and institutional fixation gives it no hallowed monuments, no revered creedal statements or unbroken successions to show the other churches; but also, and more significantly, because many of these groups have failed to make their position articulate or have, in seeking to do so, affiliated themselves either with Protestant Orthodoxy or with American Liberalism, and unwittingly betrayed the simple New Testament faith they stood for in the effort to defend it.

In view of the fact that the Faith and Order movement in its early days was largely borne by Anglicanism, and Life and Work by liberal Protestantism, both of them committed *a priori* to concepts of authority which have no intention of being content with the New Testament, a serious hearing for the Free Church viewpoint could hardly have been expected in those quarters. On the other hand, the roots of the ecumenical movement in Christian youth work, which in its nondenominational and voluntary character is a kind of Free Church, in missions and in evangelism (if John R. Mott is, through the Christian youth and missionary movements, the grandfather of the ecumenical movement, D. L. Moody is its great-grandfather), should have made such a serious hearing possible in more recent years, if the view had been adequately articulated. Missionaries found it easier to tell a Brahman or a Bushman about Christ than to ask him to jump on the escalator of Occidental cultural and ecclesiastical development at some arbitrary point half or two-thirds of the way up.

II. The Unity We Seek Is Supranational

The efforts of the Constantinian and post-Constantinian State Church were unsuccessful in maintaining unity; one after another the Donatists, the Arians, and the Nestorians, all of them incidentally more missionary than Constantine's Church, had to be splintered off. But at least the scope within which institutional peace was sought was most of the known world. The Reformation put an end to that. Convinced that separation from Rome was unavoidable, the Reformers appealed to their local princes and city-states to guarantee their survival. The result of this appeal to the state, on a local basis, to back up the breach with Catholicism, has created division ever since. One can even doubt that the difference between Luther and the Swiss Reformers would have led in the end to the formation of two separate Lutheran and Reformed traditions if it had not been for the sanctioning of that difference by local political loyalties. And even beyond this separation into two major streams, the state church system led to the creation of other groups which either refuse it for reasons of principle (the Free Churches) or were driven out of it because it could not find room for a new moving of the Spirit (Methodism, the Moravians).

It goes without saying that a church whose catechism, liturgy, and church order are determined by a state is singularly handicapped in ecumenical conversation. Even if its representatives are convinced of the wrongness of their church's position, they are generally incapable of doing anything about it.

But even more offensive is the outworking of the political *a priori* in the field of ethics, even in churches not institutionally bound to the state. It would be hard to find a more flagrant implicit denial of the givenness of Christian unity than the churches' unhesitating consent to nationalism in its demonic military form. No doctrine of Christian unity has yet explained why it should be more serious for Christians to disagree about the relative merits of episcopal, synodical, or congregational polity than for them to accept, under formal protest but with no real intention to object effectively, to prepare for, and to carry out if necessary, mass killing of other Christians at the call of their respective governments. (This is not to imply that the mass killing of heathen would be more desirable; but it is a disobedience of the field of missions rather than in the field of ecumenics).

93

This observation does not necessarily drive one to pacifism. It does mean, however, that to take seriously the fact of Christian unity as given would revolutionize the positions of those Christians who argue the necessity of war, as a last resort, for the defense of order. None of the arguments which justify morally the participation of Christians in war can justify their participation *on both sides* of a war. Ecumenical bodies have never accepted pacifism as the only Christian position; but even such apologies for war as just, or as unjust but necessary, as were recognized at Oxford, Amsterdam, and Evanston, cannot possibly provide grounds for accepting a situation in which Christians neutralize one another's efforts toward justice by fighting on both sides.

If Christians in the Allied nations were right in accepting war because the defeat of Hitler was necessary for the defense of order, then for the same reason all Christians in Germany should have been conscientious objectors. Unless it be admitted that Christian unity goes at least that far, so that even state churches admit the obligation to look the possibility of mass conscientious objection in the face and define the conditions under which the refusal of war would be just, as they have for centuries been defining the conditions under which war is just—it will not only be hard for some of the rest of us to be much impressed by the recurrent advocacy of necessary compromise, of force as the basis of order, and of war as a form of police action. It will be still harder to believe what the advocates of such measures say about their unity in Christ with their brethren who, because they were born under another flag, are now their victims.

III. The Unity We Seek Is a Discipline

It is a part of the heritage of the Reformation that, although considered essential, Christian behavior is nonetheless treated as subordinate to Christian teaching and worship. This explains the predominance of discussion of Sacraments and Doctrine in the first generation of ecumenical effort. Even more characteristic is the fact that, as ecumenical bodies do begin to open certain fields of ethical study, unity in ethical commitment is not the expressed aim. *That* it is important to be politically responsible is strongly emphasized; *how* it is important to execute that responsibility is much less clear. In most places the result is that Christians conscientiously vote on both sides of most issues, making their decisions for reasons only remotely theological, canceling one another out and making an ethical farce of the spiritual unity they confess. Many will in fact argue strongly in form of their "pluralistic" system, on the grounds that to unite on any political option, as if a moral problem were involved, would be clericalism. That Christian medical men should all express their faith through their profession would be agreed ardently by all; but if one were to ask that all Christian doctors unite in a certain attitude toward abortion, socialized medicine, or telling patients the whole truth, the response would be that such a request smacks of encyclicals.

This kind of ethical pluralism, finding its norms in a secularized concept of responsible laymanship, will not ultimately either unite Christians or make an impact on the world. It begins by assuming that the Christian layman's final ethical choice will be made, not in any particular normative relation to the center of Christian unity, God's Revelation in Christ, but rather on the basis of accepted social and axiological structures. The Christian layman according to this view will do what he does better, more honestly and more humbly than if he were not a Christian; but what he does will be what any other equally intelligent man would have done in the same situation.

The thought world of the New Testament was entirely different. Unity in ethical commitment was for the apostolic church no less central than unity in faith and worship. Christian behavior was not the lowest common denominator of a fully baptized society, but a kind of life strikingly, offensively different from the rest of the world; it dared to claim that Christ himself was its norm and to believe in the active enabling presence of the Holy Spirit.

With Christ as the criterion of obedience and the Spirit as Guarantor of the possibility of discipleship, the Church cannot but be a disciplined fellowship of those who confess that, if there be one faith, one body, one hope, there must also be one obedience; that God's Will may be known in the Church and commitment to its application expected of her members.

This New Testament view of the Church as a unity of ethical commitment might not require believers' baptism; it would at least require bringing a degree of order into the host of mutually contradictory reasons brought forth for baptizing indiscriminately the children of any one on a church roll, as well as of maintaining on the rolls people who, in awareness of what it would mean, demonstrate no intention of making their ethical decisions in the light of the gospel and in the fellowship of the brethren.

IV. The Unity We Seek Is Not a Common Denominator

Considerable harm has been done to the ecumenical cause by the oversimplification which assumes that if only the major Protestant bodies could get together the problem would be solved. Some religious journalists judge every denominational convention by two criteria: How well is the denomination digesting its past merger? and how rapidly is it moving toward the next one?

There is one truth in this oversimplification. It is true, as this view assumes, that most American Protestant denominations have no *raison d'être;* that they no longer, as denominations, stand for any distinctive principles significant enough to justify separate existence. What this attitude does not see is that, when the separate existence of two denominations is not justifiable, then their merged existence, which remains just as clearly a separate existence with reference to the rest of Christendom, and preserves still fewer distinctive values than before, is little better. *If* organizational unity on this basis *were* the real problem, the movement toward merger in the One Great (American) (Protestant) Church with a melting-pot polity and a theology chosen by the majority would have to go much faster to make any sense. Some such mergers may nevertheless be useful; but their utility and their danger are to be measured on the level of business administration, and not on the level of ecclesiology.

One reason that such mergers are no solution is that, within most denominations, merged or not, there exist differences of greater import, with reference to the authority both of Scripture and of the denominations' own traditions, than those with which the merger deals. But more serious is the fact that the common-denominator approach, be it in merger or in interchurch agencies, by channeling into one stream all the institutional inertias and by catering to the urge for centralization which is more a quirk of the Occidental mind than an ecclesiological necessity, cuts itself off from the United Church's two sources of vitality. Not only does it tend to estrange the better organized and increasingly self-sufficient "leadership" from the local congregations which are the

96

living cells of the church; it further isolates itself from the broadening and deepening effects of conversation across the whole spectrum of Christian convictions, since the concentration on middle ground (or what seems in American Protestantism to be such) loses touch progressively with precisely those groups which are convinced deeply of something or other, which do have a *raison d'être*, because their distinctive beliefs legitimately motivate distinct existence as long as they are believed and as long as schemes of unity would require their abandon. The convinced Episcopalians and the convinced Congregationalists, the Historic Peace Churches, the nondenominational fundamentalist missions, the Assemblies of God, the convinced theological conservatives and the convinced liberals, the Anglican, Eastern, and Roman Catholics—some of them, groups with an irreplaceable heritage, others of them among the fastest-growing churches of our time—must be deliberately left out of the discussion if the locus of unity is to be the attainable consensus. What threatens us at the end of this path is a sort of latter-day *Volkskirche*, a religious projection of the good and bad conscience of the American middle class, open to everybody because it stands for nothing.

The Given Unity of Christians in Christ will be given as we accept it in faith; in faith which dares take the Brother seriously to the point of grappling with him in true conversation, in faith which will love and serve him across every border to the point of subordinating (Jesus said "hating") other loyalties; in faith which will be ethically responsible for him to the point of demanding of him the same full obedience we demand of ourselves. To accept less, to believe less, than that *this* is the Unity which because it is a promise is a command as well, would be to deny the Lord.

Chapter Nine

Church Unity and Communication

Richard R. Caemmerer

Professor of Practical Theology, Concordia Theological
Seminary; Lutheran Church–Missouri Synod

My contribution to this series of articles is that of a member of
a church—the Lutheran Church–Missouri Synod—which has
stood apart from the organized ecumenical effort. "Member"
does not mean "representative." My denomination has an ex-
pressly congregational polity, and any pronouncement it might
make on church unity or any other question would be subject to
local and individual criticism. This article simply states the judgment of a person who has long had the opportunity to appraise the
attitude of his own church and at the same time the attitude of
those outside it.

In the *Ecumenical Review* for October, 1955, W. A. Visser
't Hooft undertakes to define "the unity we seek." He reaffirms
the principle that there already exists an underlying unity, but
says that the form in which that unity is to be manifested is subject to varying interpretations and experiences. The World Council of Churches, while affirming the underlying unity, avoids asking
subscription to a specific form of this unity, thereby endeavoring
to implement the search for forms which will include as many
Christians as possible in the surface unity of the church.

What is a denomination like my own saying, by implication,
about the unity of the church when it remains aloof from national
or international programs of ecumenicity? Is it saying that the
underlying unity does not exist and therefore should not be sought?
No. With all Christendom the Lutheran Church–Missouri

98

Synod confesses its faith in "the Holy Christian [and we mean catholic, in the sense of universal] Church, the communion of saints."

Does my church object to "seeking" unity? No. It takes seriously Ephesians 4:3: "Endeavor to keep the unity of the Spirit in the bond of peace." True, like all organizations composed of human beings, the Missouri Synod church finds it difficult to keep the human factors—personal phobias and jealousies, the ethnic heritage, the sociological pattern—from influencing its judgments. It is at this point, long before it engages in interdenominational or international approaches, that my church finds it necessary to clarify its own theology and set its own household in order. That it should do so is a matter not of pride but of need.

Is there then a difference of opinion concerning what form of unity is to be sought? My church has the reputation of demanding "agreement in doctrine" before acknowledging unity. Is that simply an exaggerated affirmation that "faith" is the unity we seek? Do we assume that church unity is achieved as more and more people are led to subscribe to identical doctrinal propositions?

I believe that such an assumption misleadingly oversimplifies the question of "unity in doctrine." Doubtless we of the Lutheran Church–Missouri Synod, as well as our more ecumenical friends, all need to confront the problem of what "unity in doctrine" really means. The phrase has the dignity of history behind it. It stems from the dawn of the Reformation, when the disruption of church unity in Europe prompted immediate and serious attempts to heal the breach. Article VII of the Augsburg Confession says: ". . . for the true unity of the church it is enough to agree concerning the doctrine of the gospel and the administration of the sacraments." The same article suggests that there be less concern for the things of "order": "nor is it necessary that human traditions, that is, rites or ceremonies, instituted by men, should be everywhere alike."

But what does that article really say about "doctrine"? Some think it says: "for the true unity of the church it is sufficient that there be agreement concerning the gospel and the sacraments." That is, when men accept identical propositions concerning gospel and sacraments, you have unity. When you cannot get such agreement, you don't have unity, and what is more you tend to lose interest in seeking unity.

I believe that what the Augsburg Confession is saying here is: "In order to have and perceive the true unity of the church, you must get Christians with one accord to think and work (*consentire*) for the teaching of the gospel and the administering of the sacraments." The gospel is not so much a "doctrine" or a bundle of doctrines as a message to be promulgated and applied to men. The sacraments are ceremonies which serve their purpose not so much when people agree as to what they are but when they are actually administered to people. For the church, says this same Article VII, "is the congregation of saints, in which the gospel is rightly taught and the sacraments are rightly administered"—mind you, not just rightly possessed, but rightly taught and administered, *to people*.

This may look like a bit of theorizing. Yet it seems to me that this is the heart of the problem, both of an ecumenicity that faultily seeks a faulty unity and of an anti-ecumenicity that seeks no unity at all. The former says, "We are all together already; let's look that way." The latter says, "We shall be one with you when you subscribe to our statements of doctrinal principle." There must be a saving alternative. The Augsburg Confession, to which I am pledged as a clergyman of the Lutheran Church–Missouri Synod, offers that alternative: The church is people who belong to God in Christ. Their unity is that they are held together to love, build, nurture, forgive, bless one another. What helps them to do that is that the gospel of Jesus Christ is taught to them, that the sacraments of Jesus Christ are administered to them. The gospel of Jesus Christ is at one and the same time that which they say to one another and that which moves and motivates them to say it.

In other words, this so-called "doctrinal unity" is not quite in place in a list of the "unities we seek." Rather it is a tool for achieving unity. Certainly the church of Christ should have no color line, no money test, no caste system. Certainly churches that claim to be Christian should reveal their common source in and allegiance to Christ by working together. Certainly their structures of internal government should be such as not to impede unity. But what produces these cooperative and irenic attitudes? It is right teaching of the gospel and right administration of the sacraments.

100

It is especially important that denominations within and outside the organized ecumenical movement understand each other at this point. The history of the church reveals the wide disparity through the centuries of what has passed for "gospel." The sacraments have undergone similar vicissitudes. That gospel and sacraments be "right"—this is not merely a part of an end-aim, unity, but a part of the search for unity. To possess the gospel and the sacraments "rightly" is not tantamount to seeking for unity. Gospel and sacraments must be brought to people, to the Holy Christian Church, which means all Christians. If I am content to teach my gospel and administer my sacraments just to a consciously singled-out segment of the church, I am in danger of becoming a sectary; I do not foster the unity of the church. Together with my "right" gospel and sacraments I need the outreach, the lines of communication, to bring them to others. Furthermore, all over the world there are men and women who have a word of the true gospel to speak to me. I must let down the drawbridge, tune in on their channel, so that the church of Christ may become the one body he envisioned.

Obviously my kind of denomination has more practice in keeping the drawbridge up than in letting it down. Our ways of communicating are frequently awkward, our intentions seem ambiguous, our message unacceptable. But from the other side too hampering goes on.

We are reminded not to stress our Lord's deity to such a degree that we lose sight of his humanity and so become Docetists. We need that reminder. But we do not like to see the redemption worked by Jesus Christ turned into mere sweet example.

We are reminded that loyalty to Scripture can become biblicism and superstition. We need that reminder. But we worry about the speculations that give the Bible purely human origins and so empty it that it becomes a word about people rather than a Word from God.

We are reminded that Bible and church can be set up as authorities in such a way that they vitiate the life of the heart and soul. We need that reminder. But we are concerned over the will to disbelieve and its bold presumption in setting itself up as an authority.

101

We are reminded that the gospel of the cross is "one formula, one human definition," and that we must be careful not to be sectarian in our accent on it. We need to be reminded that redemption is bigger than any doctrinal formulation of it. But we are apprehensive lest the putting of it into words silence God's plan of mercy to the world.

Suggestions to those within the organized ecumenical movement come with small grace from a person outside it. But disadvantaged as I am by experience I shall still try to say to the experienced: Be aware of our inexperience. Do not write us off as prideful; some of what seems to you pride is the awkwardness of the inexperienced. Forgive our suspicions. Respect what we are trying to do in our own household. Try to understand, even if we have not been too successful in telling you about it, what a power we find the gospel of Jesus Christ to be, and hence our will to speak and hear it well. Do not prejudge our faith as naïve because it is stated in biblical or historical forms. Help us to make good our belief in the Holy Christian Church, our confidence that where even two or three are gathered in the name of Jesus he is in their midst.

Chapter Ten

A Survey of Doctrinal Consensus and Conflict

Edgar M. Carlson

President of Gustavus Adolphus College; Augustana
Evangelical Lutheran Church. These are the results
and interpretation of a unique survey made by a group
in Minneapolis. Findings are based upon 5,704 returned
questionnaires, of which 5,162 were from laity, 272
clergy, and 270 not identified. Ten denominations and
about 700 congregations were involved.

I. ANALYSIS OF QUESTIONNAIRE FINDINGS

A. An Identification of the Major Issues

For the purposes of the survey, all major areas of doctrine were
regarded as possible points of agreement or disagreement and incorporated into the Check Sheet of Christian Beliefs. They were
identified by the following headings, followed by alternate statements which were intended to suggest doctrinal positions that
have been or are important to one or more of denominational
groups:

a) The Bible
b) The Basis of Authority Is—
c) Jesus Christ Is—
d) Salvation Is Possible Because—
e) Salvation Means—
f) The Christian Church Is—
g) The Minister or Priest Is—
h) The Sacrament of Baptism Is—
i) The Sacrament of the Lord's Supper Is—
j) Christian Unity Means—

Respondents were asked to check only one answer which "seems to you to correspond most closely to your own belief." A blank space was left for each of the areas, in which they were invited to write in their own statement if none of those suggested seemed satisfactory.

Section K offered opportunity to "check *all* the areas in which you think Christians must agree doctrinally before there can be further development of Christian unity." The purpose of this section was twofold: 1) to identify the questions considered most crucial in connection with further steps toward unity, and 2) to seek some indication of how important the respondents felt doctrinal agreement to be.

The results leave no doubt that doctrinal discussion is relevant to the ecumenical movement, especially from the viewpoint of the laity. The clergy believed that it was least important to agree on the doctrine of the ministry (15% checking this item) and the most important to agree on the doctrine of Christ (54% checking this item). The Bible and the Basis of Authority each were checked by 35% of the clergy. More than 70% of the laity believed agreement was necessary on the doctrine of Christ and almost the same percentage on the doctrine of the Bible. They also agreed that the doctrine of the ministry was least important (28% checking this item). Other suggested items were checked by approximately one third of the respondents.

The consensus seems to be that the crucial doctrinal questions for further development in Christian unity are 1) Jesus Christ, 2) the Bible, and 3) the Basis of Authority.

B. Areas in Which the Largest Measure of Agreement Exists

It must be borne in mind that no attempt was made in this survey to probe behind the words and phrases used to ascertain the meaning which was in the mind of the respondent. The Check Sheet aimed to suggest as clearly as possible certain concepts which are used more or less frequently in talking about the Christian faith and thus to enable the respondent to identify himself with a position which he considered congenial to his own views. In one or two instances, it is apparent that the statement used to define a position did not convey the intention of the frames of the Check

Sheet, and it is likely that in many specific cases the understanding of the person checking the sheet and that of the questioners did not wholly coincide.

1. The Christian Church

The statement checked more frequently by the laity than any other statement in the entire Check Sheet was "The Christian Church is the fellowship of all those who accept Jesus Christ as their Lord and Savior." (68.23%) Approximately the same percentage of clergy (67.28%) concurred, although in their case they gave larger percentages to two other statements. More than four times as many laymen preferred this statement to its nearest competitor (". . . Where the Word of God is preached and the sacraments rightly administered") and more than twelve times as many as the third statement in popularity (". . . the people of God called out of the world to be his own"). Among the clergy the nearest competitor received less than 10% of the total responses ("the community of those who have experienced new life in Jesus Christ"). Nearly 6% selected the laity's second choice and nearly 8% the laity's third choice.

The preferred definition held a clear margin in each of the denominational groups with the exception of the Lutheran and the Episcopal clergymen. In both cases, the laity approached the total percentage for the preferred definition.

2. The Ground of Salvation

The statement checked by the clergy more frequently than any other in the entire Check List was, "Salvation is possible because God, in Christ, freely offers forgiveness to all who repent and believe in him" (70.53%). This received the second largest vote of the laity (62.69%). Second place for both went to ". . . Jesus Christ has paid the penalty for our sins" (laity—25.5%, clergy—10.14%). This preference also held uniformly throughout the denominations, except that the Mission Covenant laity gave first place to the second alternative above. A significant number of Episcopal clergy (37%) preferred ". . . Jesus Christ has conquered sin, death, and the devil," and a significant number of Lutheran (33%), Evangelical United Brethren (32%), and Evangelical and Reformed (35%) laity favored the second alternative above.

105

3. The Person of Christ

The second largest response from the clergy was given to the statement, "Jesus Christ is truly God and truly man" (68.16%). This also received substantial endorsement from the laity (45.19%). Since three of the possible responses clearly implied the divinity if not the deity of Christ (the other two being, ". . . God himself, not subject to human limitation," and "God himself, choosing to come to earth in unique human form") these three total responses might well be added together as the measure of agreement with regard to the divinity or deity of Christ. The totals are then 82% of the clergy and 75% of the laity. If one adds a fourth statement which could imply divinity in a very broad sense (". . . a man approved of God who uniquely revealed the nature of God") the percentages become 95.49% for the clergy and 89.58% for the laity. Only 2.62% of the clergy and 6.02% of the laity would accept ". . . one of the world's greatest spiritual teachers."

4. The Sacrament of the Lord's Supper

Although no single response received the sort of endorsement given in the three areas listed above, the extent of the agreement was surprisingly large. Three of the responses implied communion with the person of Christ in the sacrament (". . . communion in the real body and blood of Christ," "communion in the true body and blood of Christ under the bread and the wine," "communion with the living presence of Jesus Christ"). The third alternative received the largest endorsement from the clergy (46.75%) and the second received the largest endorsement from the laity (42.32%). However, the three responses together received 68% of the laity and 60% of the clergy votes. The statement ". . . a memorial to the death of Christ" received 13.85% from the laity and 25.92% from the clergy. ". . . a symbol of participation in the Christlike life" received 14.5% from the laity and 7.4% from the clergy.

Denominational divergences are much greater in this area than in the other three, although only the Mission Covenant and Baptists, clergy and laity in both instances, give the largest response to the memorial concept and only the Congregational laity gives the largest response to the view identified as "participation in the Christlike life."

C. Areas in Which Major Disagreement Exists

1. The View of the Bible

Although the doctrine of the Bible was one of the three on which most respondents felt it was imperative to reach agreement, this was also one of the areas in which least agreement was found. The Check Sheet contained six alternatives which were as follows:

Clergy	Laity	The Bible . . .
20.52	22.21	1. . . . is the inerrant, and infallible, verbally inspired Word of God.
16.41	16.73	2. . . . is the infallible Word of God subject only to errors in transmission.
8.20	3.62	3. . . . is all the Word of God, but not all parts are equally applicable to us.
17.53	27.9	4. . . . contains the Word of God.
32.08	23.60	5. . . . is the unique historical record of God's revelation to inspired men.
2.61	3.83	6. . . . is one of several records of man's search for God.

Although there is more agreement within single denominations than within the total responses, the divergence within each denomination is more impressive than the uniformity within any one of them.

2. The Basis of Authority

Almost as wide a divergence appears in responses in this area. However, four of the responses assumed the Bible to be the authority but varied in identifying the authoritative sources of interpretation (". . . together with the pronouncements of the historic councils of the early Christian Church," ". . . as interpreted by the living Church in our time," ". . . as interpreted by each individual"). If these may be grouped together for a broader alignment of those who assert the Bible as the basis of authority, 70.15% of the laity and 63.03% of the clergy (with 15.29% more writing in their more specific statements) chose answers within this group. 19.11% of the laity and 15.6% of the clergy checked "the Holy Spirit revealed in the conscience of the Christian individual and

107

the Christian community," and 3.59% of the laity and 4.47% of the clergy checked "human reasons, as it handles both the Scripture and the tradition."

Here again, the divergence within denominations is more impressive than the agreement, although Lutherans give a rather clear margin to ". . . the creeds and confessions of the Church."

3. The Meaning of Salvation

Although there is no uniformity in the way respondents wish to speak of what salvation means, it would probably be an unjustified conclusion that there is a sharp disagreement with regard to this question. It is significant that 19.32% of the clergy felt it necessary to formulate their own statement, as did 4.64% of the laity. This was a larger percentage of individualized responses than occurred in any other section. Sixty-three and eighty-four hundredths per cent of the laity and 41% of the clergy chose responses which define salvation in specifically religious terms (". . . winning heaven and escaping hell," "living without fear of death or the burden of guilt"), and 26% of the laity and 38.63% of the clergy chose responses defining salvation in terms of the quality of life in which it issues ("being enabled to live a godly life," ". . . a way of life that is both excellent and permanent"). Only 3% of the laity and less than 1% of the clergy were willing to have it mean ". . . learning to live happily and successfully."

Denominational deviations from the general pattern of responses are as follows: Disciples and Congregational clergy responded heavily to ". . . a way of life, etc." (although laity in both cases gave equally large preference to ". . . living without fear of death, etc."); 52% of the Baptist clergy and 21% of the Baptist laity wrote in their own definitions.

4. The Sacrament of Baptism

The disagreement at this point is marked and follows rather closely denominational lines. Evangelical and Reformed, Episcopal, and Lutheran responses, clergy and laity, give substantial preference to ". . . a rite by which one is made a member of the Church of Christ." Mission Covenant, Disciples, and Baptists prefer ". . . the testimony of those who consciously acknowledge Jesus Christ as Savior and thereby renounce a worldly and sinful life" (lay members even more emphatically than the clergy in the

108

latter two groups). Methodists and Presbyterians prefer the definition ". . . a sign of membership in God's covenant people available to adults and their children" (Methodist laity deviating). Congregationalists prefer ". . . a symbol of gratitude to God and of dedication of life to him."

5. The Meaning of Christian Unity

Both clergy and lay respondents clearly reject an interpretation of Christian unity which either means ". . . gathering of all Christians into one visible church organization" (7.87% of the clergy and 11.67% of laity) or ". . . a spiritual oneness without interest in organizational co-operation" (3.7% of clergy and 3.06% of the laity). However, 50.26% of the laity and 36.57% of the clergy choose ". . . a spiritual oneness indifferent to organizational forms but based on agreement as to the fundamentals of Christian faith." The laity give second place to ". . . the maintenance of various denominations, but each mutually respecting one another's validity as churches" (23.1%) with only 7.17 checking ". . . a spiritual oneness manifested partially in organizational co-operation." For the clergy, the corresponding percentages are 18.05% and 30.09%.

Only the Episcopal clergy gave preference to "one visible church organization," but their lay members followed the general pattern indicated above. Disciples of Christ and Congregational clergy gave substantial preference to "a spiritual oneness manifested partially in organizational co-operation"; but their lay members also followed the general pattern. *It may be worthy of note that the denominations not affiliated with the ecumenical movement do not differ significantly from the rest in their conception of the desirable form of Christian unity.*

II. SUMMARY OF IMPLICATIONS

The Minneapolis Study Committee endeavored to achieve the following:

1. To inquire into the extent of theological agreement and disagreement between contemporary representatives of the various denominations.
2. To inquire into the relation between existing differences and the historic positions as defined in the creedal or confessional statements of the various church bodies.

3. To ascertain whether the apparent theological agreement in the contemporary churches may not be indifferent to theological issues.

The Committee believes that the first and third of these goals were adequately achieved and that its data can yield significant results with respect to the second goal, but it is not now in a position to submit statistical evidence toward that end.

A. The Nature of the Unity We Seek

It is clear that neither clergy nor laity feel any great urge toward organizational unity. They also disown "a spiritual oneness without interest in organizational co-operation." A substantial number of clergy respondents (30%) believe Christian unity means "a spiritual oneness manifested partially in organizational co-operation" (cf. to 7.17% of the laity). However, 50.26% of the laity and 36.57% of the clergy believe it means "a spiritual oneness indifferent to organizational forms but based on agreement as to the fundamentals of the Christian faith." Twenty-three per cent of the laity and 18% of the clergy are content with "the various denominations respecting one another's validity as churches."

It would appear that the movement toward unity cannot rely heavily on the desire for unity in the contemporary churches. It must rest on an imperative that grows out of the Christian Gospel and the very nature of the Christian faith, about which churches must become more aware than seems presently to be the case.

B. Homogeneity in Faith

Is there a homogeneity of faith among these respondents? Theological expression is not necessarily the most accurate gauge of Christian faith. How much theological diversity can exist within the fellowship of the "believers" has always been a living issue for the Christian Church. No Christian denomination, historically or currently, has completely identified a single theological formulation with the existence of faith, nor, on the other hand, asserted the complete irrelevance of theological formulation to the existence of faith. It is possible to be a heretic within every denomination.

Generally speaking, "faith in Christ" has involved a judgment concerning Christ's relation to God and Christ's relation to the believer. Christians have asserted that God was in Christ in some

110

unique sense which they have characteristically described in a doctrine of the divinity or deity of Christ, and they have asserted that he mediated to the believer the forgiving grace of God in such a manner as to be both Lord and Savior. If the essence of the Christian faith is in these two affirmations, there is very substantial homogeneity in faith among the respondents to the Check Sheet. 82% of the clergy in all the denominations and 74% of the laity chose responses concerning Jesus Christ which clearly asserted his divinity. An additional 13.48% of the clergy and 15.48% of the laity were willing to say that he "uniquely revealed the nature of God." If this be permitted to imply divinity in a more general sense, 93.48% of the clergy and 89.58% of the laity were willing to assert his divinity.

The overwhelming choice among the responses dealing with the ground of salvation was ". . . God, in Christ, freely offers forgiveness to all who repent and believe in him." (70.53% of the clergy, 62.69% of the laity.) If one adds two other responses which also assert Christ's central importance to salvation (". . . Jesus Christ has paid the penalty for our sins," ". . . Jesus Christ has conquered sin, death, and the devil"), the percentage of responses which affirm that Christ mediates to the believer the forgiving grace of God in such a manner as to be both Lord and Savior becomes 89.36% for the clergy and 93.66% for the laity.

Since our knowledge of Christ and of the faith of the early Church has come to us by way of the Bible through the Church, it is natural that our faith in Christ should also include a judgment with regard to the Bible and the Church. There is very substantial agreement among the respondents that the Bible is the "basis for authority" (70.15% of laity and 63.03% of clergy) although there is considerable divergence with regard to the authentic sources of the interpretation of its meaning. "The Holy Spirit revealed in the conscience of the Christian individual and the Christian Community" was checked by 15.67% of the clergy and 19.11% of the laity. There was surprising unanimity with respect to the doctrine of the Church, which for the large majority of respondents (68.23% of laity and 67.28% of clergy) is "the fellowship of all those who accept Jesus Christ as their Lord and Savior." This definition also underscores the homogeneity of faith concerning Christ and the ground of salvation.

111

The findings would seem to support the observation that there is a large measure of homogeneity in the faith of contemporary Christians across all denominational lines. Whether it is greater or less than that which lies behind the creedal formulations may be controversial. Did not the creedal differences arise largely in the explication of the meaning of the Bible, the Person of Christ, the Church, and the means of grace, and in the way in which these were related to one another? In some of these areas divergences and disagreements still exist.

C. Theological Concern

If the results of the survey are to be taken at face value, it cannot be assumed that the more congenial relations between denominations are the result of indifference to theological issues. When asked to check "all the areas in which you think Christians must agree doctrinally before there can be further development of Christian unity," each of the ten areas which had been used in the Check Sheet was checked by a significant number of both clergy and laity. Each item was checked by not less than one sixth of the clergy and not less than one fourth of the laity. Approximately 70% of the laity checked "Jesus Christ" and "The Bible." These two also led for the clergy though with a smaller percentage (54% and 35%).

D. The "Working Faith" of the Churches

It is assumed that the clergy represent a doctrinal position which is sufficiently close to the "official traditional formularies of faith" to be acceptable to the denominations in which they work. An attempt to establish a somewhat more rigid denominational "pattern" proved unprofitable. But a review of the accepted positions as defined by the responses of the clergy is very illumining. For instance, all of the respondents could be included in the Methodist Church without increasing the diversity which is represented by the Methodist clergy in four of the areas surveyed; the view of the Bible, the basis of authority, the ground of salvation, and the sacrament of baptism. Ninety-four per cent could join the Lutheran or Presbyterian churches without increasing the diversity in the views of the Bible which already exists in the clergy of these denominations and to that extent represents an accepted position. Approximately the same would be true

112

with regard to the doctrine of Christ and the ground of salvation. On the latter, the same proportion could also join the Mission Covenant or the Evangelical and Reformed Church. Seventy-two per cent could be Episcopalians or Lutherans on the doctrine of the sacrament of baptism, and more than 95% could be Presbyterians. Four or five possible positions on the Lord's Supper are taken by Episcopal clergy and these account for 96.38% of the total responses. On the same doctrine Lutheran clergy take two positions, Congregational clergy 3, Mission Covenant clergy 4, clergy of Disciples of Christ 2, Evangelical and Reformed clergy 1, Methodist clergy 4, Evangelical United Brethren clergy 2, Baptist clergy 3, and Presbyterian clergy take all five.

The conclusions which must be drawn from an examination of these responses is that a kind of theological ecumenicity already exists within each of the denominations. The conception of denominational doctrinal positions that are clearly defined and that constitute barriers to be overcome between the denominations is inadequate. The theological questions which are confronted in relations between the denominations are not different from those which are faced within the denominations themselves. The basic question is not the relationship of one theological interpretation to another, but the relationship of all theological interpretations to the faith which these interpretations aim to clarify. No denomination escapes this problem by withdrawal from the ecumenical movement and none solves it by participation in the ecumenical movement. The certainty of faith may not carry with it an objective certainty in its theological explication. It may be a theological gain to have had this underscored by the manifest theological diversity actually existing among the accredited clergy of even the more closely knit and historically oriented Christian communion.

E. Agreements and Disagreements

The areas in which the largest measure of agreement exists are 1) the nature of the Church, 2) the ground of salvation, 3) the Person of Christ, and 4) the sacrament of the Lord's Supper. If the sample is typical, it should be possible to make progress toward a broadly accepted view of the sacrament which would remove the barriers to intercommunion. Disagreements are evident in 1) the view of the Bible, 2) the basis of authority (particularly

113

with respect to its authenticated interpretation), 3) the meaning of salvation (perhaps more difference than disagreement), and 4) the meaning of Christian unity.

F. The Focus of Doctrinal Study

The agreement indicated on the Person of Christ and the primary position of the Bible for further development in Christian unity strongly suggests that these are the points from which to move in further doctrinal discussion. This is further underscored by the disagreement which is revealed in the views of the Bible. The unexpected agreement with regard to the Lord's Supper suggests the fruitfulness of work in this area.

G. Nonmember Churches and "the Common Faith"

The survey does not throw significant light on why some churches have remained outside the ecumenical movement and what about the "common faith" might attract or repel them. With one or two exceptions, they did not participate extensively. The Mission Covenant responses differ from the general pattern of the responses only with regard to the specificity with which certain positions are taken (e.g., their view of the Bible, of the Church, and of baptism) and others are voided. All positions taken by them are also taken by some clergy within the member churches, but not all positions taken by many of the member churches are also taken by them. The very inadequate data suggest that even as between member and nonmember churches the differences that matter are not theological.

Part Three

Unity to Be Seen and Experienced

> ... Christ Jesus himself being the chief cornerstone, in whom the whole structure is joined together ...
> —*Ephesians 2:20*

Chapter Eleven

The Unity of Spirit and The Forms of Church Unity

Langdon B. Gilkey

Professor of Historical Theology at the Vanderbilt University Divinity School; American Baptist Convention

A great many of us Christians are concerned with unity. As we have discovered, however, the definition of that unity is elusive at best. Most of our vagueness on the "nature of the unity we seek" centers around one central problem, namely, what is the relation of unity of spirit to more concrete forms of unity? By "unity of spirit" is meant probably a certain inner spiritual state toward other Christians, consisting of mutual tolerance, recognition, trust, and concern; the willingness or perhaps eagerness to co-operate in common ventures; and, in general, an absence of a sense of rivalry and a presence of a strong sense of mutual comradeship in a common cause. By "more concrete forms of unity" we mean several things, especially unity of ecclesiastical organization, unity of doctrinal affirmation (creed or confession), and unity of administrative programing and direction. The first, then, implies the intangibles of Christian community, the second the more outward and visible structures of Christian community. All of us would agree that a vital sense of Christian community among all Christians is both the divine purpose and our own goal in these discussions. Our question, therefore, is: how are these two related, or, more specifically, how much of the visible, concrete structures of unity are necessary in order that there be reality to the invisible, intangible spiritual unity?

At first it was thought that the only form of "concrete unity" relevant to the problem of spiritual unity was unity of organization and ministry—in short, ecclesiastical unity. Because, however, many groups are hesitant about church unity on doctrinal grounds, and because historically many splits have occurred in the church's life due to theological or confessional differences, it was thought helpful to encompass within this discussion the relations of spiritual unity not only to concrete ecclesiastical unity but also to theological unity. Hence the expansion of the subject of this paper.

I.

Many people feel that the spiritual unity to which we refer can exist without any of the more concrete forms of unity. Thus to them an inward sense of trust and togetherness is itself the sole goal of the ecumenical movement. They ask, "Why must we go on from here?" since some spiritual unity is already achieved in groups like this one and in the fact of the present World Council of Churches itself. Thus to them the continued existence of separate, independent, and sovereign churches is no contradiction to the reality of "oneness in Christ"; spiritual unity can exist without other more concrete forms of community.

To many, however, this is not the case. They feel that in order that there be any reality to the spiritual level of community, there must also be present certain minimal concrete forms or symbols of community. Spiritual unity cannot exist without the support of more tangible structural elements of unity and oneness. This was discovered at the inception of the ecumenical movement. Certain mission groups, who already felt some mutual trust and fellowship, found it necessary to establish structures of co-operation in their mission work. For they discovered that the mere existence of totally separate denominations engaged in the same work on the same mission field inevitably caused conflicts of work and therefore disunity of spirit. As a result, it was decided that enough concrete organizational unity to provide a unified program was necessary in order that the intangible unity of trust and co-operative spirit exist at all.

Recent ecumenical history has revealed in other areas the same interrelatedness of visible and invisible unity. In Ephesians the unity of Christ's body is described as involving at least three areas of togetherness: "one Lord, one faith, and one baptism," and we could add from many biblical sources a fourth—one mission to

118

the world. Let us discuss each area briefly in turn and see how each involves both visible and invisible, concrete and spiritual forms of unity.

One could say that the present ecumenical structure has been founded on the realization that all Christians affirm the same Lord. For it is on the basis of this common concrete religious affirmation that "Jesus Christ is God and Savior" that the spiritual unity we now possess has been achieved. A provisional unity has been accomplished on what Dr. Visser 't Hooft calls an "Erasmian basis," namely on the discovery that we are united at the very heart of our religious beliefs, and that despite our other differences all Christians share a common religious and theological basis.

When, however, one moves beyond "one Lord" to "one faith and one baptism," our visible separations of structure and of confession begin to cause disunities of spirit. There is nothing so shattering to the inward sense of spiritual unity as our dividedness at the Lord's table: at each ecumenical meeting this separateness of sacramental worship is the clearest evidence of our unachieved oneness. And many significant groups of Christians cannot even join the achieved unity of "one Lord" because they find in that unity many baptismal practices not in accord with their own. These differences of sacramental practices stem, as we shall see, from the most concrete aspects of the church's life, namely, from the character and status of its ministry and from its particular view of the meaning of church membership. And these expressions of structural disunity, whether they result in exclusion from the eucharist or in rebaptism, manifest and incite the deepest sort of disunity of the spirit.

Similarly our lack of unity in "faith," taking "faith" here to mean the content of beliefs of the Christian community, expressed in creed, confession, or "statement of fundamentals," results in an inevitable disunity of spirit. Wherever doctrinal orthodoxy is taken ultimately seriously, and this holds for great bodies of Christians, a spiritual unity is virtually impossible until a more concrete theological unity is achieved. We shall deal with this point more fully later: suffice it to point out now that it is an example of the dependence of the inward sense of spiritual community upon a more tangible aspect of community, namely agreement on the essentials of belief.

119

Finally, the outward manifestation of Christian unity in its mission to the world requires some minimal unity of programing and of co-operative work and therefore of structural organization. As the example of missionary work shows, completely independent and sovereign efforts by different church organizations inevitably foment and increase rivalry and disunity. And this is as clearly true on the local level of church life as it is on the level of world-wide outreach. If the mission of the Church to the world is to be one, if the Church is to come to the world as one community, it must achieve some tangible structures of unity and co-operation on every level lest again tangible disunities create and prolong spiritual disunity.

It seems evident, therefore, that in order for real Christian community to exist spiritually among the churches, more unity in the structural, tangible area of the church's life must be achieved. Christian unity on the spiritual level is prevented by disunity on the concrete visible level. Hence the necessity of "going on from here" as the World Council determined to do at Evanston. Now it is in two main areas that this present concrete disunity reveals itself: in the area of polity and sacramental practice and in the area of theology or faith. Here what is lacking is on the one hand a unified pattern of ministry or of orders, of organizational structure, and on the other hand a unity of confession or of theology. A brief analysis of these areas of disunity reveals that unless in the future these forms of disunity are somehow mitigated, no abiding unity of the Christian community, even on the most evanescent spiritual level, is possible. Let us, then, look more closely at these areas in which concrete forms of disunity prevent the unity of spirit.

To many Christians these things that separate us are the unessential aspects of Christianity, for we find the essence of Christianity to lie elsewhere than in either its structural form or its theological statements. We are, therefore, inclined to be impatient with those who insist on "their way" of doing or thinking at the price of Christian community: is it not, we say, narrow-minded and bigoted to emphasize traditional matters at the expense of charity? Each of us who feels that way should realize two things. First, that even we place the essential core of Christian faith somewhere (be it either in an ethical benevolence or in a vague monotheism), and that we would neither feel spiritual Christian fellowship nor achieve concrete Christian unity with a group who denied *that* essential core. And second, that these "separatist" groups are no different from ourselves in this, because each of them finds the core of Christian faith and practice to reside in exactly that structure or theological affirmation which we regard as unessential and to which we are willing to compromise. To them to compromise or to surrender that essential element is to endanger the essential religion by which they live. Although, therefore, we may disagree with them as to what is essential, it is not fair to call them either "narrow" or "traditionalists." This fact also explains why it is more difficult for churches than it is for individuals to express unity amidst genuine divergencies. The church group is the bearer of this central element of religion; a church, therefore, cannot compromise that element without fear of the irreparable loss of what it holds most valuable. An individual merely participates in this essential element; he or she does not bear it and so is not responsible for its continued existence and reality. Thus, for example, an individual Episcopalian can participate in a common communion without fear that the reality of the Christian eucharist will be lost. But were the Episcopal church to do it, many Episcopalians would rightly feel that what they take to be the essential element of the Christian religion had been compromised out of existence. When, therefore, we are discussing the permanent unity of church groups and traditions, over and above the temporary unity of individuals in this or that service or endeavor, we must remember that we are dealing with much deeper, more complex and more ultimate issues—and that it is not merely a matter of "why don't we just get together," but a matter for the deepest thought and the highest charity.

The most familiar "block" to the achievement of both visible and invisible unity among the churches centers around the polity or structural form, the orders or ministry of the church. To Catholicism in all its forms (Roman, Orthodox, and High Anglican) the essential element of the Christian religion is the grace of Christ which, through the work of Christ, is resident on earth in his body, the Church, and which is communicated to the members of that body through the sacraments of the Church. Jesus Christ founded the Church as his body on the apostles and by implication upon their episcopal successors. Thus it is through this apostolic ministry that the Church is continually re-created and constituted.

121

Without them the institution founded by Christ would not be; without them therefore the grace of Christ, which comes to the Christian through the sacraments of the Church, would not be available for salvation. Thus, wherever there is not an apostolic ministry, there is not the body of Christ, and consequently there is no valid sacrament, there is no grace and no salvation, and there can be no Christian truth. To the Catholic, therefore, the continuing visible body of Christ, the apostolic Church, of which the one episcopal ministry is the structural backbone, is the essential core of the Christian religion, and cannot for the Catholic be lost without the loss of Christian grace and salvation. For this reason, to all Catholics there cannot be the spiritual unity of the Christian community without the organizational unity of an episcopal ministry; and, as a corollary, there cannot be the spiritual unity manifested in intercommunion and pulpit exchange until all sacramental worship and all preaching stem in some way from this one apostolic ministry. Hence, therefore, in this basic problem of church unity an essential structural difference presents a block to spiritual oneness.

This particular block, however, is not confined to Catholicism. Many Protestant groups likewise locate the essential core of Christian practice in the form of the church, only in this case it is the autonomous, congregational form which they find in Scripture. To them no church can be a church of Jesus Christ unless it has this autonomous congregational form; and so, like the Catholics, they hesitate to compromise their polity lest they lose their own relation with a valid Christian worship. That structural reorganization which would create for the Catholics a valid Christian ministry, namely an inclusion of all ministries in and under an apostolic episcopal ministry, would be the very structural unity that would drive these autonomous congregations away. Furthermore, because they understand the Christian faith solely as a personal inward matter of decision and experience, any recognition of a baptism not based on an adult decision of faith or experience of grace is inconceivable to this sort of Protestant. Thus just as a sincere Catholic cannot avoid saying "no" to intercommunion, so a sincere Baptist must insist on the "rebaptism" of a converted member. And yet both these requirements perpetuate and incite spiritual disunity among Christians. In this way again the problem of spiritual unity and oneness in the church as a whole is intimately involved with concrete questions of organization and of sacramental practice.

Equally important to some groups of Christians are questions of theology and confessional orthodoxy. The liberal emphasis on feeling, experience, and behavior, and its de-emphasis on creeds and theological propositions has made many of us overlook the importance of this area. Most contemporary Christian leaders and many groups are "liberal" enough in tradition to establish Christian communion with others whose theology is vastly different— although none of us could establish the same sort of spiritual unity with those of a totally different theology, such as polytheists, atheists, or racists. To many communions, however, the essence of Christianity is its message of redemption to be found in Scripture. This "Gospel" or Word is what is received by faith, and, in that union of the Word of the Gospel with faith, a man is justified, reborn and saved. Wherever this Gospel is preached and believed, there is the Church; wherever it is lost, there the Church has been lost and salvation is unavailable to men. Thus for the reformers and their churches, the purity of the Gospel, and hence its accurate "confessional" statement, is the essential core of the Church's life; to compromise in theology, and so to lose this Gospel, is both to blaspheme God's Word and to lose the hope of salvation. For both Luther and Calvin, accuracy of faith is a duty superior to width of charity, that is, one should not establish communion with those who reject God's Word. This emphasis on orthodoxy, which is also shared in their own way by Greek Orthodox and Roman Catholics, has dominated both Lutheran and Calvinistic churches in their long history, and has come recently to dominate orthodox Protestantism in all its forms, including such groups as Baptist and the so-called Churches of Christ which are not traditionally confessional or creedal churches. To many of these churches, "spiritual fellowship" is dependent on confessional unity. And so for many of them mutual recognition, toleration, trust, and comradeship are not really possible until there is in some measure real agreement of mind on the fundamentals of the Christian Gospel. Again the concrete unity of theological affirmation is essential if the spiritual unity of Christian fellowship is to be achieved.

When one surveys these blocks to Christian communion, each of them touching some central element of the Christian religion, one becomes sadly aware that concrete areas of disunity will continue

123

for some time to prevent the fullness of spiritual unity. Surely it is clear that these problems are not merely those of tolerance versus bigotry. Rather they are issues that lie on the deepest and most serious level of Christian commitment so that only a true renewal of the Spirit and a genuine transformation or rebirth of Christian groups can accomplish the unity of the churches. We should also remember, however, how much has been gained; how vastly the liberal movement has effected the conquest of even Protestant confessional divisions by Christian tolerance and charity; how the development of neo-orthodox theology has begun to bridge the gap between liberal and conservative Protestant theology; and finally, how the recent rediscovery of the wholeness and oneness of Christ's Church has brought even Catholics into a consciousness of their obligation to search for a wider Christian unity.

One final point needs to be made. It is interesting to note that the greatest force for spiritual unity is apparently a sense of common membership in an historical communion with a common history, a common message, and a common saving power. This is not so much a matter of conscious doctrinal agreement as it is of organic participation in one community in which one lives creatively and so which claims one's loyalty. It is this organic sense of community and solidarity which is the central source of denominational power and loyalty, and which is the basis for reunion within a single denomination after organizational or theological differences have caused division. Certainly if we are searching for the clearest manifestations of this elusive concept of "unity," it would have to be this sense of participation in, and loyalty to, an organic community bound together by its common tradition and heritage, a common history, a common way of life, and a common hope of salvation.

It is also plain that this sense of common participation and loyalty to a community rarely, if ever, manifests itself beyond the denominational level. It is experienced by each group for itself, but it is not experienced by the church as a whole. And we can well ask why this is so. Is not the whole Church of Christ, the invisible communion of saints, a more ancient and more august body than any of the denominations? In the broadest sense does it not have a common heritage, tradition, and message despite its differences (and every denomination has differences within it)?

But plainly there is no comparable vivid consciousness of this organic unity of all Christians in one community.

The reason, I feel, is that there have been for the whole Church no such concrete patterns of unity, no structures of visible unity, on which the vivid, powerful, and binding experience of common membership can build. Where there are visible symbols and structures of unity, as in every denominational group—be they confessional agreement, sacramental unity, or unity of Christian practice—there "flesh" is provided for the incarnation of the spirit of unity. But where these symbols and structures of unity are absent—as they have been in the divided Church—any powerful spiritual sense of community is inevitably absent, too. For as this survey has emphasized, not only do doctrinal and organizational differences in themselves represent vast disunities of spirit, but even more, the mere fact of organizational separateness itself incites a spirit of rivalry and partisanship which makes impossible the development of Christian oneness.

Our own conclusion would be, first, that for the sense of spiritual unity the small beginning of organizational unity within the World Council is of the utmost importance. And second, it appears that further minimal forms of concrete unity beyond the World Council level must be achieved if any real spiritual unity is to be realized. Surely these further stages of concrete unity must include, first, a more unified and so mutually recognized ministry so that intercommunion and mutual recognition of baptism is possible, and so that pulpit interchanges can be more frequent. Second, it must encompass enough mutual theological agreement and understanding so that confessional differences neither divide nor exclude groups from each other. And finally it must involve enough common co-ordination of policies and programs so that the churches encounter the world in their mission to all men as one Church, unburdened both by inner rivalries and costly duplication. These minimal structures of unity do not at all involve uniformity or centralization. Rather, as we have tried to show, they provide the necessary visible "flesh" in which the spirit of uniting love may dwell—for ours is a world in which the divine love becomes incarnate only when it takes on the humble garment of flesh.

Chapter Twelve

The Distinction between Church Order and Organization

Eugene R. Fairweather and David W. Hay

Eugene R. Fairweather is Associate Professor of Dogmatic
Theology and Ethics, Trinity College, Toronto; Anglican
Church of Canada

David W. Hay is professor of Systematic Theology, Knox
College, Toronto; Presbyterian Church in Canada

I. THE VISIBLE CHURCH AND ITS ORDER

The problem of "church order" can arise at all only because the
Church is essentially a visible society, ministering the invisible life
in Christ to human persons who live in space and time. The
Church is a visible reality because the Word of God was made
flesh to bring life and light to men.

> The life was made manifest, and we saw it, and testify to it, and pro-
> claim to you the eternal life which was with the Father and was made mani-
> fest to us—that which we have seen and heard we proclaim also to you, so
> that you may have fellowship with us; and our fellowship is with the Father
> and with his Son Jesus Christ. (1 John 1:2-3.)

It will be universally agreed that the mysterious reality of the
Church's life—fellowship with the Father and with his Son Jesus
Christ—is accessible only to the vision of faith. The Church is
the fellowship of the Holy Spirit, whose free and invisible working
can be discerned only by spiritual insight. The life of the Church,
like the life of each of its members, is "hid with Christ in God"
(Colossians 3:3), and faith alone can see the Church for what it
is: the bride and body of Christ. At the same time, this secret
truth of the Church's life is not simply transcendent and supra-
historical; on the contrary, earthly, temporal creatures are enabled
to share in it through visible, historical media, and this, too, is

recognized from one end of Christendom to the other. Whether we focus our attention on the proclamation of the Word, the administration of baptism, the celebration of the Eucharist or the maintenance of ministerial order (papal, episcopal, presbyterian, congregational), we are bearing witness to the common conviction that the existence of the Church in time is bound up with certain historical institutions whose roots lie in the divine purpose and action. Visibility and historicity are not accidental to the life in Christ, but integral and essential. It is not just that an essentially invisible fellowship of totally unidentifiable Christians somehow finds fortuitous expression in indifferent outward forms; at the very least, we shall need to affirm that God through his chosen media—e.g., the Word and the sacraments—calls men into the common life of the Church and sustains that life through time.

It would, of course, be idle to pretend that all Christians understand the visibility of the Church in the same way. To begin with, we differ in our identification of the factors which constitute the historical *esse,* or being, of the Church; but further, this diversity may be at least partly rooted in different views of the relation of the visible fellowship to the hidden life of the Church. Some will argue, for instance, that through the Word and the sacraments God calls men and gathers them into a fellowship of believers which exists prior to and independently of its outward ordering and constitution, and further, will emphasize the fact that this fellowship, while real, is not visible in its true reality except to the all-seeing eye of God and the trust of human faith. On this showing, while visible media are the ground of the fellowship, the latter, as a fellowship of true believers, known to God alone, cannot be thought of as itself taking essential, visible form, except insofar as it must make *some* provision for the continued preaching of the Word and administration of the sacraments. Others will be concerned to assert the significance of the visible community, made up of the baptized and, perhaps, further marked by a more or less clearly defined hierarchical structure, as the essential embodiment of the fellowship of Christians in Christ. On this showing, the visible fellowship and its essential activities—e.g., its eucharistic worship—will be a "sacrament" or efficacious sign of the Church's hidden nature as the body of Christ.

We must not minimize the seriousness of the wide diversity of our correlations of the visible and invisible in the Church, of which the two examples given can hardly be more than samples. Indeed, it is not too much to say that this diversity at its widest stands for radically divergent estimates of the significance of outward and visible signs as instruments of the Spirit. No one, of course, can or will deny that the outward forms are dead apart from the lifegiving presence of the Spirit. But some will think of the historical structure and life of the Church as at once the normal instrument and the sole adequate expression of the Spirit's sanctifying power, while others will tend to see in the historical forms mere vehicles which God, in his sovereign freedom, uses to accomplish his gracious purpose. In other words, for some people participation in the wholeness of the visible fellowship will be part of the very meaning of the communion of the Holy Spirit, while for others the correlation of inward and outward will be a simple relation of spiritual power to chosen instrument. At the same time, we must observe that all Christians, however variously they may interpret the correlation of Spirit and form, will find it necessary, in formulating their ecclesiology, to take serious account both of the invisible grace and of the visible signs as factors in the making of the earthly, historical church.

In considering the visible aspect of the one Church, however, we shall soon discover that a distinction must somehow be made between the visible means by which God continues his Church in being as the Church and the transitory social forms whose nature it is to come into being and pass away under the pressure of historical change. On the one hand, the wide diversity of such things as liturgical and administrative forms, of which every student of church history must be aware, makes it plain that very few of the external structures known to history can be universally necessary for the historical existence of the Church. On the other hand, the very visibility of the Church as a continuously identifiable society in history requires some outward forms as enduring elements of its historical structure. While the Church lives by the invisible power of Christ and his Spirit, it lives in history as the people of God, created by God through the decisive events of the Old Covenant and re-created in the death and resurrection of the Word-made-flesh, and it can scarcely lack all historical connection with its historical foundation. Thus the distinction which for our present purposes has been formulated as a distinction between "order" and "organization"—between the universal and the limited, the permanent and the temporary—forces itself on our attention. But this is just the beginning, and only careful analysis will establish and clarify the distinction and determine the principles of its application to particular customs or institutions.

II. The Problem of Order and Organization

The discussion thus far has brought to the fore several closely related questions, which may be summarized as follows: (1) Is it possible to make any significant distinction between "order" and "organization," which will really hold when applied to some particular element of the Christian tradition? (2) Granted that some such discrimination is possible in principle, in what terms are we to make it in practice? (3) Is the concept of "apostolicity" at least one of the criteria by which we must be guided in any attempt to work out the distinction? This section will deal with the first question, while sections III-IV will consider the second and section V the third.

Obviously the fundamental issue is the possibility of making the distinction in any clear and definable way. It has been argued, quite rightly, that unless order is to be thought of as abstract and invisible—in other words, in self-contradictory terms, since it is the visible form of a human community with which we have to do—it must itself be pictured as a kind of organization. The problem, then, is really one of distinguishing between a "primary" organization (or "order") and a "secondary" organization (or "organization" *simpliciter*)—i.e., between an ordered structure which at all times and in all places serves as the means by which God constitutes the Church as the Church, and an organization which under particular circumstances gives effective expression to some aspect or other of the primary structure. In other words, we are looking for the principles of discrimination between such a primary organization as is essential to the continuous existence and identity of the Church as a visible society and the variety of administrative structures through which this "order" can be made operative.

The possibility—indeed, the necessity—of such a distinction can be shown with the help of a reasonably neutral example. The essential order of the Church includes the celebration of the Lord's Supper, or Eucharist, as one of the sacraments of the Gospel of Christ. For the action of the Church to be identifiable as the

Eucharist, it will be commonly agreed that it should be celebrated with the elements used in its prototype, the Last Supper, and that the sacred meal celebrated with these elements should be further identified and designated as the Eucharist by an appeal to the original institution, provided, however, that whatever usage or customary pattern is followed conforms to these minimal requirements, no particular liturgical rite can be regarded as essential to eucharistic order. It may be highly desirable—in fact, the majority of Christians would probably regard it as desirable—that the identity of each Eucharist with the continuous sacramental life of the Church should be fully expressed by the use of a form which embodies ancient tradition and historic usage and in this way explicitly reflects the common mind of the Church. But such full acceptance of the ecclesiastical tradition is not of the *esse* of eucharistic order; indeed, many will argue that it may involve a distortion of the primary meaning of the Eucharist, while none will be prepared to make a particular liturgical form an essential condition of sacramental validity.

It is just the distinction illustrated here that must be applied all along the line if we are to avoid two opposing errors: (1) the "Platonizing" of order out of existence by making the distinction between order and organization absolute and total, and (2) the enslavement of the Church under any and all conditions to an elaborate organizational pattern regarded as sacrosanct. To affirm and defend such a distinction in principle is, however, only the beginning of our analysis, and we must go on to explore the nature of the distinction more fully, as a prelude to its application to certain issues which may affect contemporary church relations.

III. Order and Function in Society

The use in the New Testament of such terms as "people" (*laos*) and "members of the household" (*oikeioi*) to refer to the Church and its members suggests the inescapable analogy between the Church as visible, historical community and the other social groups in which men live. The family, in particular, whose essential functions are readily definable in relation to fundamental human needs, can be considered in such a way as to shed more than a little light on the character of the Church's visible structure, and more especially on the distinction between order and (secondary) organization. As we shall see, it is true that the family as universal human

130

institution does not provide a complete parallel to the unique historical community of the Church. Indeed, it should be emphasized that no human community or combination of human communities can provide more than a secondary key to the mysterious meaning of the Church's invisible-visible reality. Nonetheless, the family does illustrate at least one aspect of our problem, and there may well be some advantage in beginning our search for the required solution outside the Church and in isolation from the particular ecclesiastical interests and conflicts which have made it necessary for us to try to make explicit the primary principles of church order. Other examples might, of course, have been chosen from social life—e.g., the performance of the essential functions of government under any one of a wide variety of constitutions—but some social example has necessarily to be chosen, if the meaning of the Church's historical, social, visible life is to be clarified, and the family, as a universal human institution, rooted in the creaturely nature of man, seems likely to provide the most comprehensive analogy.

The regulation of family life in the institution of marriage is an instance of what we have referred to above as order or primary organization. Unless we are simply to equate marriage with sexual union, on the ground that the physical act is the same in marriage and in promiscuous sexual relations, we shall eventually find it necessary to define marriage as an ordering of biological sexuality with a view to certain specifically human functions of sexual union. By way of a preliminary description, at any rate, let us define this ordering of sexuality in marriage as twofold: (1) the placing of sexual intercourse in the context of mutual responsibility between human persons; (2) the extension of this responsibility to the care and nurture of the human persons who are born as a result of sexual intercourse. On this showing, the minimum definition of marriage, which will distinguish it from casual cohabitation, must involve the recognition of marriage as an ordered relation between husband and wife (or perhaps between husbands and wives), which in turn directly implies an ordered relation between parents and children. Over against this essential order, we can set a variety of organizations (patriarchal, matriarchal, egalitarian, monogamous, polygamous, and so forth), which may more or less effectively serve the functions of marriage in particular cultural, social, or economic situations. This kind of contrast between order and

131

organization should be readily intelligible, because it is rooted in real and visible distinctions—between marriage (order) and promiscuity (disorder), on the one hand, and between perceptibly different patterns (organizations) of the marriage relationship, on the other.

Of course, it is obviously true that all this still leaves us with the problem of surveying the boundary between the essential order of marriage and the varying social forms which it may take without losing its identity. In other words, what is primary (order) and what is secondary (organization) in marriage and the family as such? Just because there is no absolute opposition between order and organization, since both are tangible, external patterns, the problem is a complex one. There will arise, for instance, the question of the relation of marriage as such to monogamy. Some might argue that by its very nature marriage is inherently monogamous, because it is only in such a relationship that the sexual union of a man and woman is placed in an order of real mutual responsibility. On this supposition, plural marriage would essentially be legalized concubinage, a mere simulacrum of true marriage. Others might reply, however, that while sacramental, Christian marriage—the *plene esse,* the full being, of marriage—is inherently monogamous, because of its mysterious likeness to the union between Christ and the Church, the natural, functional responsibilities of marriage can be fulfilled in a polygamous organization of the family. Such conflicts as these are important enough, but it should be emphasized that difficulties and divergences in the application of our principle do not negate the principle itself. Both theories of marriage referred to above treat it as an ordering of sexuality in terms of certain functions, in contrast to a disordered sexual activity, and both agree further that this order can be embodied in a variety of organized domestic economies without losing its identity. It is to this essential distinction between constant *function* and diversified *embodiment* that we may usefully look in searching for the principle of discrimination between *order* (or primary organization) and *organization* (in the narrower, secondary sense).

IV. Order and Function in the Church

Our next task is to sketch the application of this principle of discrimination to the problem of order and organization in the Church itself. We may begin by emphasizing the parallel between the Church and the family, even if we shall soon have to go beyond it. The Church has to do with the fundamental relation of man to God, just as the family has to do with the primary relationships between human persons. But just as the casual sexual intercourse of a man and a woman does not in itself constitute a marriage between them, so the mere meeting of human beings to think or talk about God or to say prayers does not suffice to constitute them into a church. On the contrary, the Church is a creation of the triune God. It possesses and is partially defined by a divinely given order, in which man is related to God on the basis of God's action. That order is constituted by certain functions, through which, by the sanctifying action of the Holy Spirit, a man's faith and hope and love are effectively related to the God of revelation, just as through the functions of the order of marriage a man is effectively related to wife and children. If we approach the problem of church order in this way, it can be argued that there are three distinguishable functions which together define the essential order of the Church—provided always that we recognize on the one hand that the Church depends on the powerful presence of the Spirit for the efficacy of its ministrations and the true significance of its fellowship, and remember on the other hand that the Word and sacraments are God's appointed means of grace within the visible fellowship of his Church.

A. The Church must preach the Gospel of God's action, toward which Christian faith is essentially directed. Christians may, indeed, differ in their understanding of the role of preaching in the work of man's salvation. While some will see in the sacraments the means of a unique communication of the divine life, others will regard the preaching-teaching office as no less communicative of Christ's person and work than the sacramental office. But all will agree that apart from the confession and proclamation of the Gospel, the Church must lack one of the primary elements of its functional order.

B. The Church must administer the sacraments, in which the divine action in history is mediated to men through visible, tangible signs. Without these efficacious signs of the grace which sustains the Church and the Christian in faith and love, the Church would lack another essential element of its functional order.

133

C. The Church must necessarily be maintained as a visible fellowship, in and by which the Gospel is preached and the sacraments are administered, and through which human communion with God is expressed and shared. Some may think of this visibility of the Church as realized in the acts of proclaiming the Word and administering the sacraments. While they will not ignore the significance of the government or discipline of the Church as a visible society, they will emphasize the congregation of the faithful, which finds its center and its continuity in Word and sacrament, as the essential, ongoing, visible reality. Others, however, will insist on the role of the visible Church of a particular ministry which is authorized by God to preach and to teach, to administer the sacraments, and to govern and order the Church, and will see in such a ministry an essential element in the functional order of the Church. Without trying to minimize differences among Christians at this level, we should presumably agree that, apart from the divine call to certain persons to perform these kerygmatic and sacramental functions in the congregation, the Church would not exist as an ordered community, so that the entrusting of the ministerial function to particular persons within the fellowship is an element of church order, distinct from the Gospel which is proclaimed and the sacraments which are administered. This agreement does not, however, extend to the general recognition of a ministry ordered in any particular way as essential to the common life of the Church, nor does it involve any unanimity of understanding as to how the authorized ministry is related to the congregation of the faithful.

All that has been affirmed in the last four paragraphs amounts to saying that the Church is constituted by God, Father, Son, and Holy Spirit, through a particular order which distinguishes the Church from every other "religious society," and further, that this order consists of the Gospel, the sacraments, and the ministry of Word and sacrament (however broadly the notion of "ministry" may be defined). Over against this essential *order* we should set the variety of possible *organizations* through which these constant functions may be performed under varying conditions. The Gospel, for example, must be propagated and interpreted by the use of a particular catechism or confession, or by some other medium which serves to present the Gospel in certain historical circumstances, but can never be simply identified with it. Similarly, the sacraments must be administered according to some particular usage or other, if they are to be administered at all, but the Christian sacrament of baptism means baptism administered according to *some* rite which embodies its essentials—not baptism administered according to Lutheran usage, say, and no other. Similarly again, the ministry must be maintained in the Church according to the usage of particular churches, if it is to be maintained at all—and since it is a distinctive gift of God for the building up of the body of Christ (cf. Ephesians 4:11ff), the calling of some to perform ministerial functions must continue if the Christian community is to endure. But the maintenance of the ministry means its continuation according to *some* usage which embodies the essentials of the ministerial vocation—not ordination administered according to the Anglican rite, say, and in no other way. In each and every one of these cases there seems to be a clear distinction between the function which remains constant through a variety of embodiments—requiring some embodiment, but not bound to any one in particular—and the particular organized expression of that function in a given time and place. To proclaim the Gospel is to declare the very basis of the Church. To administer the sacraments of the Gospel is to build Christians into the Church on that declared foundation, through their putting on of Christ in baptism and their participation in the eucharistic *anamnesis,* or remembering, of his death. To commit these correlative functions to the authorized ministry within the Church is to emphasize their nature as corporate acts of the Church rather than individual acts of Christians, and to exhibit the corporate character of salvation in Christ. But all this is very far from saying that Gospel, sacraments, and ministry are to be bound to any particular theological, liturgical or administrative forms as to be incapable of expression in different categories, rites, or polities. It may be that further consideration will lead us to define somewhat more precisely the character of Gospel, sacraments, and ministry as constituents of the essential order of the Church, but no definition that obliterates the distinction between the enduring function and its transitory embodiments is theologically or historically defensible.

It is true that here, as in the case of the family, we face a difficult task when we come to survey the boundary between the essential order of the Church and its varying organizational expressions. The question of the relation between ministry and episcopacy is an obvious example. As everyone knows, answers to this question may range all the way from the affirmation that episcopal ordination is essential to the ministry itself, through the claim that it gives fullest expression to the meaning of the Christian ministry and the milder suggestion that it is a historically tested and venerable institution, to the assertion that episcopacy (at least when presented in terms of sacramental order rather than mere administrative organization) distorts the meaning of the ministry— for example, by negating the parity of ministers or by usurping the rights of the congregation. Once again, however, there is no reason why disagreement in the application of the relevant criteria should make us scrap the criteria as useless, if the kind of distinction we are trying to make seems inescapable. We should remember, for instance, that the most determined "episcopalian" is able to recognize the compatibility of a wide variety in organization and administration with the essential principle of episcopacy, as he understands it, while the most rigid "congregationalist" can describe a variety of administrative arrangements through which the essential ministry of the Church may be constituted and exercised. That is to say, whether those who apply it always recognize it or not, the distinction between constant *function* and diversified *embodiment* would seem to be widely operative in fact.

V. The Question of Apostolic Order

The analogy between family and Church appears to have given us at least a partial criterion for the making of that distinction between order and organization which has seemed to us to be inescapable. There are, however, certain features of the essential and constant functions of the Church which suggest that a fuller criterion is needed. More precisely, the inherent reference of the preaching and sacramental actions of the Church to the divine action in history implies that there must be a historical element in our definition of the Church's functional order. Once the radical difference between family and Church which this signifies is recognized, it will become clear that the analogy between marriage and the family and the Church is inadequate, even for the limited purpose for which we have been trying to use it. Marriage is an ordering of a universal human instinct in the interests of universal human functions. The Church, on the other hand, while its mission is universal, corresponding as it does to the universal human need for communion with God, is the visible setting of a kind of communion with God established by a particular historical revelation. Its function is to communicate the effects of that unique divine action in history which we call the Gospel of Jesus Christ—to proclaim that Gospel-history in its preaching, to represent it in its sacraments, and to maintain a fellowship rooted in that history and devoted to its proclamation and "extension." That means that the analogy between family and Church has to be, so to speak, "particularized" so that we think in terms of a given family, distinguished from other families by its traditions and its physical continuity. Of course, in view of the unique meaning of the Church's life, even this particularized analogy will ultimately prove inadequate, but it may at least carry us a step forward in our understanding of the peculiar features of the problem of order and organization within the Church.

With this in mind, we can go on to observe that in the case of the Church functional order is grounded in the "apostolic tradition," which embodies the particular historical revelation from which the Church's universal mission springs. This is clear enough in the case of the Gospel proclamation itself; the Church's message is not a generalized affirmation of divine activity in nature and history, but a witness to God's saving work in Christ. Consequently, the Church functions as the Church only when it confesses the Gospel, and not just the Gospel as set forth or interpreted in any way at all, but the Gospel as proclaimed and presented in the apostolic *kerygma,* or proclamation, and the apostolic Scriptures. For some, the canonical Scriptures as the Word of God will be the comprehensive norm of the Church's confession of the Gospel, while the use of creedal formulae may play a part in a corporate witness which must also include the preaching and hearing of the Word in the congregation. For others, the creed will be a partially independent witness to the "shape" of the apostolic *kerygma*—a creedal *regula veritatis,* or rule of truth, like that to which Irenaeus and other early Fathers appealed as a kind of "key to the Scriptures" and a safeguard against false exegesis. (The use of developed creeds in the age of the Ecumenical Councils and the later use of dogmatic decrees, confessions of faith or articles of religion, as the medium of more or less authoritative doctrinal definition on the part of the Church, is a different matter, since it raises the further problem of the relation of apostolic tradition, wherever located, to ecclesiastical authority.) Beyond this difference of attitude toward extra-biblical witness to the Gospel, we should also note the existence of other significant differences, at least of emphasis; some, for instance, will regard the encounter of man with God in the preaching of the Word as the heart of the Church's function of proclaiming the Gospel, while others will lay greater stress on the corporate witness to the Word in authoritative definition and instruction. But all are concerned with the primary principle to which both "apostolic" Scriptures and "Apostles' Creed" bear witness—namely, the unique position of "apostolic tradition" as the visible foundation of the whole structure of Christian belief, worship and life, and all will agree that the apostolic witness pertains to the essential order of the Church, just because the Church's function of proclaiming the Gospel is defined in terms of the apostolic proclamation of the Gospel.

The same principle applies to the Christian sacraments. The sacraments exist to communicate the saving work of Christ, not to express or transmit abstract spiritual values. Consequently, the Church functions as the Church only when it administers the sacraments, and not just any sacraments, but the sacraments instituted by God and transmitted to each successive generation from the apostolic Church itself. The apostolic "signs," then, pertain to the essential order of the Church, just because the Church's function of celebrating the sacraments is defined in terms of the divinely ordained "representation" of the events to which the Gospel bears witness.

The same principles apply to the "apostolic ministry," even though more complex questions are forced on us in our actual situation, confronted as we are with radically opposed conceptions of the role of the ministry in the Church. The basic questions here have to do with the kind of ministry which the Church must have if its fellowship is to be truly a *koinōnia tōn apostolōn*—a community bound together in time and space by its dependence on Christ and his apostles. The problems of the relation of the call and authority of Christ to the instrumentality of the Church, of the respective roles of historical continuity and of the contemporary community in the authorization of the ministry, and of the necessity or otherwise of a particular historical form of ministerial order, should all be noted as relevant to the broad issue. Assuming for our purposes that the call of Christ and the instrumentality of the Church cannot be completely isolated from each other, we may usefully consider certain typical theories of the way in which the Church's instrumentality is exercised.

A good many of those who are concerned with this general problem will argue that the true continuity and essential unity of the Church's life are to be found in the Gospel proclaimed and in the sacraments of baptism and the Lord's Supper observed, and that the ministry is quite simply a function of the community thus constituted. That some who share this general position would prefer to speak of "ordinances" rather than of "sacraments," and would in effect regard the administration of baptism to "believers" alone as a matter of order, should not be allowed to obscure the fact that the acceptance of this basic interpretation of continuity, unity, and ministerial authority cuts across certain otherwise significant confessional divisions. The adoption of this view will not mean that the importance of visible fellowship under properly constituted leadership is overlooked in the definition of church order. It will mean, however, that the actual constitution of the ministry in a particular Christian community may legitimately be determined by that community in response to contemporary needs and under the guidance of the Holy Spirit, since no one form of order or type of ministry will be regarded as essential or even normative for the Church.

Others, on the contrary—and this disagreement would seem to be one of our deepest divisions in the area of church order—will see an authoritative ministry, distinguished from the community as a whole and with a commission which is in no sense mediated by the congregation, as normative for (or perhaps even constitutive of) the common life of the Church. Those who think in these terms will see in the apostles of Christ the prototype of all public ministries in the Church, and will think of the contemporary ministry as in some way possessing certain elements of apostolic authority. Furthermore, some of them, at least, will find in the primitive Church an apostolic pattern of the ministry, to which the later Church is bound to conform. These concepts of apostolic authority and apostolic order will further be said by some to involve a ministry historically continuous with the apostles and apostolic authority, and this will commonly lead to the assertion that the required historical continuity is uniquely maintained by God through the episcopate and the succession of episcopal consecration.

There will also, however, be those who maintain something of a mediating position. For some, the succession of presbyters will seem an adequate medium of ministerial continuity. Furthermore, many who believe that Christ has appointed an authoritative ministry within the Church will assert that the ministry is also, in part, representative of a ministerial charge laid by Christ upon the whole body, and will draw from this the conclusion that the ministry is not so tied to an historical chain of officers that it cannot at need be reconstituted from the body of the Church according to the apostolic norm contained in the Scriptures.

Theology and history would appear to be inextricably interwoven in the assessment and defense of these divergent views. Those, for example, who regard forms of ministry as a matter of secondary organization rather than primary order will stress the absence of any biblical record of dominical or apostolic directions for the establishment of a specific ministerial order or orders or for the maintenance of the Christian ministry by some kind of sacramental continuity. Reading the somewhat scanty evidence for the period between the close of the apostolic age and the universal establishment of "monarchical episcopacy" in the light of this fact, which will seem to them to have significant theological implication, they will stress the diversity of polities within one church as the most obvious conclusion from the available evidence. Others will see decisive significance in the fact that the terms *episkopos* and *presbuteros* are used in the New Testament for the same office, and will assert that, once the apostles' unique commission came to an end, there was essentially only one ministerial order in the Church—namely, the ministry of Word and sacraments—which is normative for all succeeding ages, although at times minor differentiations may appear within the one episcopate-presbyterate. Still others will maintain the necessity (or at least the normative character) of the episcopally ordered threefold ministry. They will start from what they regard as the significant fact of the apostolic commission and, without denying the ambiguities of the historical evidence, will argue that the same second-century Church which witnessed to the apostolic Scriptures of the New Testament canon also witnessed to the episcopate as continuing those elements of the apostolic authority which were at once transmissible and permanently significant, and that this "apostolic succession" has been transmitted ever since by a process which included episcopal ordination.

Arguing along another line, those who question the significance of ministerial continuity as such will observe that episcopacy, with which the strictest views of such continuity are most widely associated, has not in fact guaranteed either purity of doctrine or the proper interpretation of the apostolic *kerygma* or the right understanding of the sacraments or of church unity, and will go on to ask what special value it can have as a symbol or instrument of the Church's unity and continuity. The defenders of episcopal order may or may not regard this as a fair assessment of the achievements of the episcopate in the history of the Church, but they will not regard its rôle in the maintenance of doctrinal purity as the sole criterion for determining the significance of episcopal order. Rather, they will argue that the episcopal succession is necessary for the Church's visible continuity—or at least is a major factor in the maintenance of that continuity—as not just a religious family but the apostolic family, in which the *koinōnia* of the apostles with Christ is extended through the centuries. They will suggest that to dismiss this kind of continuity as unnecessary and to locate true continuity exclusively in the identity of the Gospel proclaimed and of the sacraments administered is to forget that the function of the Church is not simply to maintain an identical message or to perform identical actions, but that these identities are ultimately inseparable from the maintenance through history of a visible fellowship—a community whose functional order as a visible society also includes a specifically social principle of continuity and identity. Even if the necessity of social, historical continuity is granted, however, it may still be denied that such continuity rests even in part on a ministerial succession, in addition to the continuity of message and action, or it may be argued that, whether or not such transmission of ministerial authority is necessary or important, the ambiguity of the primitive evidence—or, alternatively, its positive witness to another type of church order—makes the particular idea of the devotion of apostolic authority through episcopal succession untenable.

And so the argument will continue. But, while the diversity of doctrines of church order at the level of the ministry is obviously such an irreducible diversity as to make any compromise formula impossible, we may perhaps claim at least that there is a common substratum on which all views ultimately rest. This common ground can be stated in the proposition that the Church functions as the Church only when it maintains the ministry, and not just any ministry, but the true Christian ministry which Christ wills for his Church and to which the apostolic tradition bears witness. However divergent our interpretations of the apostolic tradition and of the will of Christ to which it testifies, we do not question the necessity of the ministerial function of the ordering of the Church as a visible society.

It is time to sum up this discussion of the apostolic Gospel, the apostolic sacraments and the apostolic ministry. As we have already indicated, the precise relation of the grace of the Holy Spirit to the media which he uses is interpreted in different ways. Some Christians, for instance, stress the general necessity and normal obligation of the means of grace, while for others the freedom of the Holy Spirit in making use of the visible means is the dominant idea. That will mean, in turn, that there will be disagreement as to the sense in which order can be described as "fundamental" to the Church. Nonetheless, it seems obvious enough that the Church has certain functions which it must perform in obedience to its Lord and apart from which it cannot rightly claim to be the Church, while at the same time it is clear that a wide variety of modes of performance is quite compatible with the integrity of the essential functions. Going on from this point to attempt an application of the distinction between primary function and secondary mode, we may suggest that the criteria of *functional order* and of *apostolicity,* taken together as our principle of discrimination between order and organization in that unique human institution which, in the hidden mystery of its life, is the body of Christ, will lead to certain preliminary conclusions. We shall be led by these criteria to recognize that, while catechisms, liturgies and polities (in the sense of arrangements for church government) belong to the sphere of organization, the apostolic tradition of doctrine as embodied in Scripture (and, according to many, in the creeds as well) belongs, together with the sacraments and the ministry, to the Church's fundamental order. This order must inevitably find expression in a more or less explicitly organized pattern of instruction, worship, and government, and we can never expect to find order in a state of naked innocence, unhampered by the clothing of secondary organization. Nonetheless, it is the visible body of order as such that belongs to the *esse* of the Church as the people of God in history, while the organization can be changed again and again without touching the esssence of the Church's divine mission.

VI. Apostolic Order and Ecclesiastical Authority

So far we have simply tried to formulate a theoretical distinction between "order" and "organization," by distinguishing the constant functions of the Church, rooted in the self-revelation of God in Christ, from the continually changing ways in which those functions are actually carried out in the ongoing life of the Church. It is obvious, however, that another question must be raised and discussed before we can pretend that the problem of order and organization has been comprehensively considered. This question has to do with the actual relation of order and organization in the Church at any given time, and it may be stated in some such terms as these: What role, if any, does ecclesiastical tradition or the authority of the living Church play in determining the organizational forms in which apostolic order is to be expressed? In other words, are patterns of organization simply a matter of the opinion or preference of particular churches or groups of Christians, as the image of body and clothing used at the end of the preceding section might suggest? Or are they, on the contrary, subject to the authoritative judgment of the universal Church and bound, at least to some extent, by its continuous tradition? Put in this way, the question is obviously a live one for Western Christendom in particular. On the one hand, the "Ultramontane" often seems to identify order and organization, insofar as he relies on the "living voice" to the apparent exclusion of any effective appeal to apostolic tradition as transcending the thought and practice of the Church in any later generation. On the other hand, the more drastically individualistic type of Protestant tends to see the identification and interpretation of apostolic tradition as the work of the individual Christian, face to face with his Bible and secure in the freedom of a Christian man. Others, notably Anglicans and "confessional" Protestants, strive in a

143

variety of ways to define some kind of *via media* that will temper without destroying the relation of the Christian to authority and law.

In the light of our earlier discussions, we may set aside for the moment the extremes of Ultramontanism and isolated individualism. Accepting, then, the broad distinction between order and organization, while noting at the same time that organization is a matter of the common life of the Church, we may tentatively suggest that certain distinctive conceptions of the actual relation of organization to order, corresponding broadly to diverse theories of the nature of social continuity in the Church, deserve our consideration in this study. On the one hand, we should observe that an emphasis on apostolicity as definable simply in terms of the abiding identity of the Gospel preached and the sacraments administered is naturally associated with a deep reserve toward the idea of the binding authority of the living Church in the interpretation and declaration of apostolic tradition. The more definitely the concept of apostolic authority as at least partially continued by way of "apostolic succession" is excluded, and the more sharply exclusive are the claims made for the canonical Scriptures as the repository of apostolic tradition and authority, the less room there will be for a notion of authoritative dogmatic teaching and the more sweeping will be the claims made for the right and duty to work for the constant reformation of the Church by the Word of God. While an excessive individualism, which would dissolve the public teaching of the Church into a mass of private opinions, is eschewed, we may note a strong tendency to think of the Church's common life as based above all on the acceptance of a common confession of faith, to which individuals give their assent in the light of their own reading of Scripture or on the basis of the exposition of Scripture by an authoritative teaching ministry. On the other hand, attention should be called to the natural parallelism between the view that certain transmissible elements of apostolic authority are really continued in the succession of bishops and the acceptance of the authority of the episcopate as the definitive interpreter of Scripture in the Church. The more comprehensive the claims made for the apostolic succession, and the stronger the sense of visible unity and continuity as centered in the episcopally ordered ministry, the less room there will be for the exercise of private judgment in the interpretation of apostolic tradition and the more restricted will be the possibilities of radical "reformation." While a simple authoritarianism, which would vest the right to express the mind of the Church in an infallible individual or an automatically infallible group, altogether apart from the consent of the Church, is avoided, the exponents of this doctrine of ecclesiastical authority commonly suppose that the solemn and considered judgment of the Church, as expressed in the dogmatic definitions of an accepted ecumenical council, is irreformable, while its canonical legislation—e.g., in the area of liturgy and polity—is reformable only by "due process."

These alternative views of ecclesiastical authority, as outlined above, are better understood as tendencies and not as clear-cut dogmas held by two solid blocs of Christians. Broadly speaking, the former view is characteristic of classical "Protestantism," while the latter view belongs rather to non-Roman "catholicism"—the terms being used for convenience, and without prejudice—but many who share these general attitudes would not regard our summary statements as adequate formulations of their respective doctrines of authority. Even these broad outlines, however, will serve to indicate that the actual relation of organization to order is quite diversely understood in modern Christendom. To take up our earlier metaphor once more, for some organization will be like a garment, changeable at will for another, while for others whose view of the Church's continuity lays greater stress on social continuity the choice of organizational garment will be governed more or less fully by ecclesiastical tradition.

The significance of this cleavage for the concrete problems of Christian reunion can scarcely be overestimated, since those who stress the "Protestant" critique of all traditional authorities will tend to think of the building of the external form of a united church as in greater or less degree a work of construction *de novo,* provided only that the foundation of essential order (whatever its exact definition) is preserved; while those who emphasize the continuity of "Catholic" tradition will be more inclined to think of reunion as the reintegration of fragmented communities into the "wholeness" of the ongoing historical life of the Church. In effect, then, we seem to be confronted with two interpretations of that "catholicity" which should determine the direction of our efforts toward Christian reunion. On the one hand, according to a view which was in possession for more than one thousand years of Christian history, "catholicity" involves participation in a common life shaped by a historical tradition which is itself grounded in and continuous with the apostolic tradition. On the other hand, according to a view which has challenged the former interpretation and historical tradition itself in the name of a recovered apostolic tradition, "catholicity" demands the perpetual reformation of the Church in the light of the apostolic Gospel as declared in Scripture. Neither of these attitudes can be overlooked in a realistic appraisal of current approaches to the concrete problem of order and organization.

VII. Church Order and Catholicity

The diversity which we have noted in the interpretation of the concept of "catholicity" does not mean that the notion is simply equivocal. However, it is understood in different theological contexts, it always includes the idea of a standard or norm of authentic Christianity, grounded ultimately in God's self-revelation in historical action. Moreover, as a normative concept, it inevitably raises the question of the status of any Christian communities which in some serious way fall short of the accepted standard. The kind of answer we propose for this question will obviously determine our understanding of the unity which, as we generally suppose, already exists among Christians despite more or less serious differences in order and organization, and this understanding will in turn influence our approach to the problem of realizing our unity more adequately in the visible common life of the Church.

Here as everywhere in the area of church order, the way in which the question is approached will be determined by one of two characteristic attitudes, both of which should be taken into account, despite the mutual suspicions of their exponents and the impossibility of reconciling them completely as they stand. On the other hand, where there is more or less of an emphasis on the necessity of the historical norms, more or less similar problems arise, which may all be summed up in this question: What is the relation to the *Una sancta* of a community of professing Christians in which one or other of the elements of "catholicity," as we have come to understand it, is lacking? Whether we are

146

Orthodox or Roman Catholics, considering the situation of Christians who are out of communion with Constantinople or Rome, or Anglicans wrestling with the question of the ecclesiastical status of nonepiscopal communities, or Protestants trying to understand the position of nonsacramental bodies, such as the Society of Friends, we shall find that to stress the significance of visible order is to be driven to face what we might call the theological problem of "church" and "sect." On the other hand, where it is believed that almost the whole stress ought to be laid on the action of the Holy Spirit, this way of putting the question must inevitably seem alien and misleading. The implicit assumption that determinative weight must be given to visibility and historicity—even beyond the unique period between the incarnation and Pentecost—will be regarded as so much defection from the essential spirituality of the Christian faith. In this context, the basic criterion for the acknowledgment of genuine "churchliness" in any Christian community must be the possibility of recognizing the fruits of the Spirit. Perhaps a brief attempt at the concrete illustration of these divergent attitudes will help to bring out the point more clearly.

Without prejudicing the obviously debatable issue of the true content of normal church order, it may be useful to choose a typical Anglican idea as an example of the first approach to the problem—if only because it is fairly widely held. According to this view, which is derived more or less directly from the "branch theory" popularized by the Tractarian Movement, while the Roman, Orthodox, Anglican, and Old Catholic Churches are branches of the Catholic Church, such bodies as the Methodist and Presbyterian Churches are simply aggregations of Christians, having no more of a churchly character than the Y.M.C.A. Such an estimate is obviously based on a real concern for the visibility and continuous historical identity of the Church. It is true that critics whose concern for the maintenance of visible continuity and unity is no less urgent have found it impossible to draw the line between "Catholic" and "sectarian" so sharply as to exclude from any part and lot in the Church of Christ a community which lacks some element of fundamental order. These critics will argue that the real power of Christian faith and the manifest signs of Christian life in communities which, from the critics' own standpoint, are radically defective, makes it next to impossible to deny that such bodies possess *vestigia ecclesiae,* or, as we might freely translate it, residual elements of true churchliness, which make it possible for them to perform some at least of the functions of the Church for their members. We should note, however, that this qualification of the more rigid doctrine does not, of itself, lead to the conclusion that it can scarcely matter much whether we receive the Christian tradition as a totality or in bits and pieces. The idea of church order as a functional whole, apart from which the One Holy Catholic and Apostolic Church would lose its identity, remains paramount, and the problem of the churchly status of a body which lacks some element of apostolic order is seen as the question of its relation through its partial order to the existing, historical wholeness of the Catholic Church. Thus the criticism and qualification of the "branch theory" still remains within the framework of its basic principle of the primary importance of integral church order.

It is this very principle, however, which is radically challenged by the second and more "spiritual" approach to the problem of "catholicity." Without simply repudiating the historical forms, but insisting on their complete subordination to the activity of the Holy Spirit, who transcends all historical patterns, those who hold this view will assert that the norm of integral Christianity should be expressed in terms of the presence of the Spirit, dynamically and personally conceived. While Word and sacrament within the ordered fellowship will be respected as ordinary means of grace, attention will be concentrated on the end rather than the means, and the reality of authentic church life will be recognized wherever it is believed that the life of the Spirit is displayed. Moreover, many Protestants will naturally move from this positive affirmation to a critique of the alternative position, with its strong emphasis on visibility and continuous historical identity, as exemplifying mere "formalism" and "unspirituality." As a result, the "Catholic" who, from his own supposedly secure position, either denied outright the churchly status of certain communions or laboriously vindicated for them a minimal reality as "churches," will find himself brought under "Protestant" judgment and defended at best on the ground that the life of the Spirit has not quite been smothered by the proliferation of external forms. Perhaps this reversal of values will be for many the most striking expression of the attitude whose first question will have to do, not with the fullness of historic church order, but with the fitness of any given order or organization to express, here and now, the transcendent power and free working of the Spirit.

Stated thus sharply, these two standpoints must seem irreconcilable, as we have already suggested. We should be careful, however, neither to accept them at one another's evaluation nor to overlook the possibility that both of them may frequently be distorted or restricted in their presentation by controversial considerations. So, for example, those who emphasize the integrity of visible order should not be accused of ignoring the power and life of the Holy Spirit, since the ultimate reason for their concern with historic order is their conviction that God intends that order to be the sacramental instrument of the Spirit. Similarly, those who stress the freedom of the Spirit should not on that account be accused of indifference to the historical and visible, since at least part of their purpose in asserting the presence of the Spirit as constitutive of the Church is to help us, in making use of the visible signs, to apprehend the divine power and love whose real means of grace they are. Obviously, there is a danger on the one hand of supposing that God has so bound his power to the sacraments and to the other visible signs of the life in Christ as to be unable to communicate that life outside the visible communion of the Church, understood in the most rigorous sense. Equally obviously, there is a danger on the other hand of undermining the Christian truth of the real, visible, historical existence of the Church, grounded in the saving acts of God, wrought out in flesh and blood. It is clear that an adequate interpretation of church order will have to avoid these one-sided errors. But it is also plain enough that no interpretation of church order can be called adequate unless it manages to take full account of the truth to which, in their very distortion of it, these partial ideas bear witness.

Chapter Thirteen

Protestantism Is Ready *Now* to Become One Church

Charles Clayton Morrison

Former editor of *The Christian Century;* Disciples of Christ

The ecumenical movement for the unity of Christendom operates in three zones: (1) on a world scale, concerning itself with all Christian churches throughout the world; (2) in a middle zone, concerned with the churches of continental Europe and the West; and (3) in Western Protestantism, concerning itself with the denominational churches of the United States and Canada, including their younger churches in foreign lands. The problem of achieving Christian unity is, in essence, the same in all these zones, but different in the degree of their nearness to or remoteness from the goal. On the world scale the difficulties are greater. In the middle zone they are substantial but less. In continental America such progress has already been made that the goal of One church can actually be envisioned.

Here the churches not only participate in the world-wide ecumenical movement, but have developed an ecumenical movement of their own. During the past fifty years, the sharp edges of sectarian claims and feelings have been worn down by the experience of many forms of co-operative association, including national and community federations. In these associations they have discovered that the evangelical faith which we all share in equal measure transcends all our differences and dwarfs them into irrelevancy. Thus the way would seem to be open for Protestantism in this zone to become One church.

I. The Greenwich Plan

Already some sixteen mergers of denominations, by twos or threes, have been achieved and other such unions are contemplated. One of these represents the *rapprochement* of eight or nine denominations under the so-called Greenwich Plan[1] for their organic union. This plan presupposes that Protestantism has now reached the stage in the development of its own inner or spiritual unity where a united church can be realistically projected. In my own words, I would interpret this presupposition as follows: *The treasures of all our evangelical churches—their doctrines, their polities, their fellowships, their very habits of doing things—can be taken up and embraced in One church without compromise of conscience or the restriction of Christian freedom.* This faith is ultimately derived from Christ the Head of the Church. But, happily, its realism is confirmed by the concrete evidence of a firm trend in Protestantism in the direction of its realization.

The present stage in this movement has been reached and illuminated by a progressive series of changes in the spirit and practice of the denominations over the past two or three generations. These changes point distinctly, I shall affirm, in the direction of a united church. Whether Protestantism is ready to become One church is a question that is being answered for us by the denominations themselves. They have reached the point where their separation can no longer be reasonably defended.

II. A Firm Trend Toward Union

It is important that the ecumenical movement in this particular zone shall take account of the actual present state of mind of the denominations. Where this is not done, the discussion tends to wander off into bypaths of irrelevancy or into depths of theological or ecclesiological theory which cloud the real issue and obstruct the open road. I shall name and discuss seven of these ecumenical commitments of the denominations. Taken cumulatively, they call imperatively for a definitive commitment to a united church.

A. *We are all agreed that the members of all our churches are Christians, equally accepted by Christ as members of his Church.* There was a time when we could not assume a unanimous and

---

[1] The Plan is the outcome of five years of study by officially appointed representatives of nine denominations. While it is projected for these denominations, it goes beyond them and could include the whole of evangelical Protestantism. It has not yet been made public, but is in the hands of the appropriate commissions of the participating churches.

hearty approval of this affirmation. It was not openly denied, but it was often ambiguously affirmed with qualifications and reservations. That ingenious theological device called "the uncovenanted mercies of God" was brought into play to cover the embarrassment of those whose sectarian conscience inhibited a hearty acknowledgment that members of other churches stood before God on an equality with those of their own "true faith." Happily that spirit is with us no longer.

B. *All our denominations are by intention, conviction and in fact equally Christian churches.* Not one will claim to be more Christian than others. It is still somewhat difficult for some to make this affirmation, but it is impossible for them not to make it. It used to be hard for Baptists to affirm it and for Episcopalians and for Disciples of Christ. We squirmed and talked about the *esse* and the *bene esse* of the church, and about immersion-baptism, and about the freedom of the local congregation from "ecclesiasticism." But we have changed. And when the ghost of these dead controversies appears and tells us that by making this acknowledgment we would deny the faith of our fathers, we are not scared. We no longer pray the Pharisee's prayer, but like the publicans, we present ourselves and our denomination before God in a spirit of humility.

A larger faith, a sensitivity to the values possessed by other churches and a more Christian humility have taken hold of our hearts and driven out the evil spirit of sectarian pride.

C. *All our denominations share equally in the sin of maintaining schismatic churches.* It is a truism of the Christian faith that schism is sin. Who did sin—the fathers of your denomination or the church from which they broke away? We cannot and need not know. It may have been the dissidents, or it may have been the church which they renounced, or the wrong may have been on both sides. But there is always sin in schism. "You are carnal," says Paul, when you divide Christ's body. Schism is not the kind of sin that is covered by the Ten Commandments, or by any social standard. The secular mind does not understand why schism is sin. Schism in the Body of Christ is a Christian sin. For the Christian conscience to be comfortable in it betrays an insensitivity to the nature of our holy faith and of the church which enshrines it. All our denominations, yours and mine, are

152

caught in this indisputable equality in the sin of schism. As Archbishop Temple said, "So long as any of us are in schism, all are in schism."

Where is the locus of this sin? Is it in our theological differences or our different modes of worship or our different forms of church order? No. There is no sin in these diversities. Indeed, there is virtue in them, and they can enrich the fellowship of a united church. Our sin lies in our maintaining separate man-made *churches* based upon them. How may we hope by God's grace to be absolved of this sin? There is only one way: *We must cease being churches.* We must trustfully offer to the fellowship of the whole church what we call our "distinctive witness" to the Christian faith. This is Christian unity. This spells a united church.

D. *Our way of thinking about the Christian faith has undergone profound changes in the past half century.* It is necessary now to look at our denominational differences in terms of their actual contemporary reality, not merely in terms of their historical origin. Yet when we are asked to state what our denomination "stands for," do we not turn to the history books where we find only what a long time ago it "stood for"? The fallacy here is obvious. The ecumenical movement is not concerned to unite the churches of a century ago; it is concerned to unite the living churches of today. These churches have all passed through an era of profound change in theological thinking and in their evaluation of the very issues out of which our denominations arose. So true is this that if any one of our evangelical denominations were not now in existence, few if any of its members would feel any urge of conscience to start it or restore it.

If this fact were seriously taken into account by the ecumenical movement it would save endless discussion of matters that are irrelevant to the concrete problem of a united church. I do not agree with that shallow view of Christian unity which scorns theology and theological discussion, and insists that it should have no place in the united church. On the contrary, my view is that a united church is the true place for the consideration of the great themes to which theology is devoted. We will always have a sectarian theology as long as we have sectarian churches. An ecumenical theology is one of the most urgent desiderata of the Christian faith. But we can achieve an ecumenical theology only within an ecumenical church.

No doubt, the conversations in the world-wide zone of ecumenical operation require long and patient consideration of theological and other ideological subjects. Conversation between the churches of East and West is clouded with mutually unfamiliar ideologies. A common universe of discourse has to be attained before there can be much talk about unity. But the denominations of Protestantism already enjoy a common ideology. Long isolated within narrow denominational walls, their main conversation with one another in the past was in the form of debate. But their mentality has now been liberated into the open spaces of common evangelical Christianity, and debating has ceased because there is so little between them that is vital enough to argue about.

E. *The doctrinal differences which formerly existed between the denominations are now embraced in the denominations themselves.* In this degree our denominations are themselves becoming ecumenical! If a denomination can embrace a considerable variety of differences on traditionally controversial subjects, and also certain innovating interpretations of modern thought on things both old and new, is it not about ready to go into a united church? My answer is that it would be more at home in the united church than to continue living with itself! This is because a denomination that has become ecumenical minded still retains its sectarian creed or confession of faith. Whether this is explicitly formulated or stereotyped in an ideology, it operates in the same manner. Thus the ecumenical spirit of such a denomination must live in constant insecurity lest a factious element seize upon its long quiescent sectarian creed and in its name divide the church. But the united church would openly embrace these various confessions of faith without standardizing any formulation or stereotype. Thus the major cause of schism would be removed.

An instructive fact to be noted in this connection is the virtual passing of the heretic. Since the days of those famous "heretics"— Swing and Briggs and McGiffert and Foster and Gilbert and Thomas, to name no others—the legal apparatus of ecclesiastical sectarianism had become rusted with disuse. But it was recently called into play in the state of Wisconsin to convict as heretics three young ministers of devout evangelical faith who deviated from the wording of a confession of faith formulated more than 400 years ago. I cannot believe that the whole United Lutheran Church, except these three young ministers, has been impervious to the light which modern evangelical thought has thrown upon the issues for which these men were convicted of heresy. But this is not my point. What I want to say is that if the Lutheran tradition were embraced in a united church, its supporters would be freed from the legal necessity of resorting to an inhumane, self-righteous and grossly un-Christian method of maintaining its sectarian integrity. They would find themselves in a context for dealing with such "deviations" in a humane and Christian manner.

The momentary situation in Congregationalism presents a pathetic but ludicrous absurdity. Instead of a denomination pronouncing a verdict of heresy upon some individuals, a factional minority pronounces the whole denomination heretical! The Congregational denomination has been second to none in its more than a half century of unanimous commitment to the cause of Christian unity. A score of years ago, it actually united with another denomination. Its own inner unity was maintained throughout the Fundamentalist storm of the 1920's, with no appreciable loss or disturbance. But now the unexpected has happened. Congregationalism has produced a Fundamentalism of its own! A minority group takes for itself the title "Association for the Preservation of Congregational Principles." It charges the whole denomination with apostasy and would forbid 75 per cent of the local churches to exercise their congregational freedom by uniting with another denomination. This is the ultimate irony of denominationalism. It re-enacts a procedure that stains the whole history of this unholy system.

But these two instances do not nullify the fact that the differences between our denominations are now largely embraced by the denominations themselves. Rather, they illuminate it (1) by the humiliation with which these anachronistic procedures are regarded by the main body of opinion in the two denominations concerned, and (2) by the demonstration that so long as the denominations exist as *churches,* these shameful disloyalties to Christ are bound to recur.

F. *Our denominations are now beginning to see that their differences, such as they are, can be more hopefully reconciled within a united church than in sectarian isolation.* The great delusion that has obsessed our denominations is that a separate *church* is necessary in order to bear witness to some Christian truth which is held distinctively. By "bearing witness" is meant persuading the general church to accept it. This delusion has always been cherished by all our denominations. Should we not now be able to learn from our history how false it is? What denomination has contributed its "distinctive truth" to the whole church by this means? Has Presbyterianism? Has Lutheranism? I know of no more tragic illustration of this fallacy than the long and stubborn separation of the Lutheran and Reformed churches. Vital differences they seemed to be four centuries ago. But because these two branches of the Reformation were isolated from each other behind the walls of separate ecclesiastical churches, they have not been able to see that the truth of one is not opposed but complementary to the truth of the other.

Have the Congregationalists made an impression upon the rest of the church by their sectarian illustration of the autonomy of its local churches? Have the Disciples and the Baptists made an impression upon Methodists and Episcopalians by bearing a sectarian witness to immersion-baptism? Have the Episcopalians made any impression at all upon the other churches of the Reformation by holding their historic episcopate in sectarian exclusiveness? Away with this shabby rationalization! To build a sectarian wall around a Christian truth does not "bear witness" to it—it takes that truth out of circulation. Prejudices are raised against the adoption of any Christian treasure offered with a sectarian patent on it.

G. *The association of our denominations in national and community federations has led them into a mode of co-operation which is, in principle, organic.* When the practice of "comity" was first proposed for application to the foreign and home mission fields, some denominations sensed a "danger" in it and refused to participate. However, it was innocent enough. It practically meant nothing more than an agreement to stay out of one another's territory. This was nearly fifty years ago. Today, however, the problem of Protestantism in American cities has become acute by the decimation of what is called the "inner city" and the mushroom growth of suburbia. The federated denominations sense the scandal that would ensue upon the mad rush of sectarian self-interest into these lush fields. Operating not by a self-denying contractual agreement among themselves to stay out of a community first entered by one of them, they commit the whole of unchurched suburbia to their federation, to allocate specific communities to specific denominations and aid the development of their churches therein.

If we take a good look at this procedure, we cannot miss the organic principle of united action by the denominations in establishing one another's churches. So long as comity meant only a negative self-restraint, it was, as I have ironically said, "innocent" enough. But this blessed innocence has now grown into a conscious organic ecclesiastical unity at *this one point*. If the denominations can co-operate in establishing one another's churches, what becomes of their special "witness" by which they have immemorially justified their sectarian separateness? Their special witness is manifestly either held with indifference or its possession by the general church is acknowledged.

Other instances in this category could be added. I will refer to one more, namely, the Federated Theological Faculty of the University of Chicago. Four denominational seminaries have created an organic union of their faculties to study and teach theology and train candidates for the Christian ministry. These seminaries represent Baptist, Congregational, Unitarian, and Disciples of Christ denominations. Their united faculty is presided over by a Lutheran dean. It includes Episcopal, Presbyterian, Reformed, Quaker, and Lutheran professors in addition to those representing the four federated denominations. The primary inspiration of this unique development is the ecumenical spirit. What it means as an illustration of the new mind in Protestantism, your imagination will make it unnecessary for me to elaborate.

III. AT THE POINT OF DECISION

The changes that have taken place in our denominations have brought us a long way on the road to unity. We now stand at the place where decision must be made. The spirit of Christ who has opened our eyes to the evil of our divisions and ameliorated our differences to the point of their relative indifference, will not let us stand gazing idly into space. I offer the foregoing evidences as marking a distinct progression, both logical and historical, toward one and no alternative goal. We may hope that this American study, prompted by the Oberlin Conference, will not bog down in theological or ecclesiological theory which no doubt

157

is relevant in other zones of the ecumenical movement but irrelevant in the scene of American Protestantism. *We are ready to become one church.* Protestantism is in quest of a church that both transcends the outworn denominational system and embraces all its treasures in one body.

The unity we seek stands in contrast to the idea of a "monolithic" church, a conception which is often imputed to the advocates of church union. I do not know of any representative Protestant churchman who conceives of the united church as consisting all of one piece. Such a church, if it could be achieved, would be quickly broken by internal pressure into many pieces. We seek no such unity. Rather, our goal is an inclusive church, rich in the variety of its thought and practice and its sensitive concern for the freedom of its members under Christ. In a word, a church in which variety is a virtue no less than unity.

Our churches have come a long way in our sectarian wanderings. But the road we have taken in the past half century has brought us together in sight of the shining tableland which is our goal. An upward path stretches clearly before us. And the light that streams upon it is reflected from the face of Christ who stands with outstretched arms.

Part Four

Unity in the Local Community

"To the church of God which
is at . . ."

—*1 Corinthians 1:2*

Chapter Fourteen

Christian Unity in the Local Congregation

Charles D. Kean

Rector of the Church of the Epiphany, Washington,
D. C.; Protestant Episcopal Church

Christian unity refers to the essential nature of the Body of
Christ. The task of reuniting the fragments of the Christian
Church is thought of not as attempting to develop something new,
but rather of restoring in visible form what has been basic to the
Christian faith since New Testament times. To talk of Christian
unity seriously means first of all, therefore, to explore theologically
the doctrine of the Church.

The local congregation derives its peculiar meaning from the
Christian faith to which it bears witness and the Holy Catholic and
Apostolic Church which it represents on the local scene. While
the parish church can be studied from the viewpoint of sociology,
and while comparisons may be drawn between the customs and
traditions of neighboring local congregations of different denominations, the real point will be missed unless congregational life is
first of all looked at in terms of theology—the doctrine of the
Church.

Effective programs designed to develop greater concern for
Christian unity on the level of the local congregation presuppose
some shared understanding on the part of those involved of the
theological significance of the congregation as the Body of Christ.
An approach that is primarily pragmatic is in continual danger of
sentimentality, irrelevance, and irresponsibility. We begin with
the doctrine of the Church.

161

The doctrine of the Church has begun to come into its own as an important part of the Christian faith in its fullness. This development in some ways appears to mark twentieth-century Christianity as distinctively as the Christological problems marked Christian faith and practice in the fourth, fifth, and sixth centuries. While there are a number of reasons for the awakened concern for this aspect of Christian doctrine, the development of the movement for Chistian reunion bears a large share of the responsibility.

To become aware of the need for Christian reunion, regardless of whether this is rooted in theological reflection or in the practical difficulties of community relations, is to be thrown headlong into a consideration of what the Church is for which unity is being sought. Yet at the same time, some share in the credit for this new awareness of the importance of the doctrine of the Church must be given to other forces in Christian life today. The growing concern for a more adequate program in Christian education, for example, has forced many church leaders to explore deeply what they are educating people for and what are the real educational influences which affect their lives. The same thing might be said about the work done by many thinkers in developing a twentieth-century apologetic for the Christian enterprise.

In any event a consideration of the doctrine of the Church is a basic part of all creative Christian thought and action today; and this is particularly true of the movement for Christian reunion. Likewise, any mature consideration of the meaning of congregational life today cannot help but lead one to think both of the doctrine of the Church and the problems of Christian reunion. Perhaps a triangle is the best symbol to use to describe the situation—with the doctrine of the Church at one point, congregational life at another, and the unity movement at the third. If one starts from any point seriously, he is eventually forced to take the other two into his thinking. If one seeks to develop any realistic program of study or action at any point, he cannot avoid dealing with the other two before he has gone very far.

One of the most unique contributions of the Jewish-Christian tradition to man's religious understanding and practice is the concept of the congregation as the normative expression of the life of the Church. This is something radically different from anything developed by the other world religions. Whether we are dealing

162

with the synagogue or the parish church, we are confronted with the fact that both exist to make possible a continuing life in which the faith and the ethic are brought into contact with the actual relationships which people have with each other in daily affairs.

One cannot understand either Judaism or Christianity without taking congregational life into account, because neither is primarily a system of intellectual beliefs, even though both have their theological formulations. Nor is either primarily a moral code, even though both point to ethical applications. Rather both Judaism, at least since the Babylonian captivity, and Christianity ever since its beginning, have been first of all fellowships of people sharing a common life and fulfilling a mission to the world.

Because of this, the congregation has been a central and necessary part of both religious thought and practice. It is more than incidental machinery. It is rather integral to the religious process itself, and without it neither the Jewish nor Christian religions would be themselves. In Christianity the congregation from the very beginning has served the purpose of making overt and concrete in particular local situations what this fellowship with a mission to the world may mean.

The First Epistle of Peter describes the Christian Church: *"But ye are a chosen generation, a royal priesthood, an holy nation, a peculiar people; that ye should show forth the praises of him who hath called you out of darkness into his marvellous light: which in the past were not a people, but are now the people of God"* (2:9). This beautiful and poetic phrase is meant to be dramatically lived out in congregational life, wherever Christians are associated with each other as part of the family of God. It is not a picture of some "invisible church" transcending the conditions of time and space but never concretized anywhere.

While the passage lays an obligation upon the local congregation to fulfill in visible form and in a particular place the mission of the Holy People of God, it does not, however, disassociate the local congregation from the Holy Catholic and Apostolic Church. An awareness of congregational responsibility does not necessarily lead to a congregational polity, but rather to a deeper appreciation of membership in the universal Church of God which is expressed locally with all seriousness but which can never be realized in its fullness in any one situation.

In the Epistle to the Philippians (3:20), St. Paul draws an analogy between the *politeuma*, the responsible ethnic subdivision in a Greek city, and the role of the Christian congregation in its community. It seems he also has reference to the Roman device of the *colonia*, the settlement of groups of retired soldiers with their families in a particular municipality to serve as a social leaven. The Christian Church is both *politeuma*, in the sense that the community can expect responsible action from it, and *colonia*, in the sense that it is supposed to influence the community in turn.

In other words, the nature of the Church as the Body of Christ becomes explicit in congregational life—where it becomes possible for people not only to speculate about the meaning of divine love but also to reflect it by loving one another as persons, where it becomes possible for men and women to know what forgiveness means because under the influence of Christ they both give it to each other and receive it from each other.

The congregation, on the other hand, has no meaning apart from the larger life of the Body of Christ, the Holy People of God, of which it is the local representative. While it may have the task of concretizing in particular situations what is true about God's relationship to his children everywhere and the resulting relationship of these children to each other, the congregation is merely the local manifestation of a reality which cannot be limited to particular times and places. Christ is the universal Lord of the Church rather than the Lord of unrelated churches. Congregational life is derived from this fact and bears witness to its truth.

Congregations may exist as the spearheads by which the Christian Church as the Body of Christ, as the Holy People of God, comes into dynamic contact with the world, but actual congregations only represent the Holy, Catholic, and Apostolic Church indirectly. Their relationship with it is through the particular denomination which established them and sustained them and to which they are expected to give their loyalty.

Congregations on the local scene are the expressions of denominationalism in all that word implies. The scandal of Christian division becomes blatant in particular communities where neighbors can co-operate with each other only to a limited extent because their church loyalties are different, and where the Christian witness in community affairs is confused by competing voices selling the same or at least very similar products under different labels.

Congregations in the downtown sections of great cities, in suburban communities, and in the smaller cities and country towns, may differ from each other in the same locality along lines having nothing to do with denominational sponsorship. One parish may emphasize its pulpit, another its educational program, and another its community ministry of Christian service. Congregations even within the same denomination may appear to compete with each other or to be presenting widely differing emphases. Yet the fact remains that, in spite of all of these differences, the local congregation regardless of its denominational allegiance appears to be offering its community essentially the same services and resources as its neighbor on the next corner.

But the answer to the problem will never be found by encouraging congregational disloyalty and irresponsibility. There is no way by which the local congregation can make contact with the Holy Catholic and Apostolic Church except through its parent denomination, and to try to by-pass what exists is to move into a world of fantasy. There are local churches which call themselves ecumenical, but regardless of their good intentions, they are really parishes with a congregational polity which choose to disavow any larger loyalty and which choose to disregard the meaning of previous allegiances in welcoming new members. Where the local congregation on its own tries to become an agent of the Body of Christ, the Holy People of God, without any reference to the existing structure of church life, it seems to be adding new divisions rather than healing old ones.

The local congregation does have an important role to play, and if it does not play it nothing much will happen as a result of unity negotiations on the level of the higher councils of the denominations. But this role is not to ignore the existence of the parent denomination but rather to articulate in every possible practical way on the local scene the meaning of the negotiations which are already under way. It does not mean to jump the gun and consummate ecclesiastical marriages on the local scene without benefit of denominational blessing, but it does mean to make a serious effort in those areas of experimentation which have been authorized and where local action will be responsible.

In the experience of this writer, the greatest obstacle to the unity movement, however, has not been the irresponsibility of local congregations by going off half-cocked, even though this does happen a little. It is rather the irresponsibility of local congregations in the form of paying no attention to the unity movement in their own denomination, to say nothing of that in the larger world around them. More programs to arouse interest in Christian reunion and to develop steps by which unity may be achieved bog down at the grass-roots than anywhere else. The opposition of those who resist proposals on theological grounds is nowhere near as serious as the inertia of those who do not care.

In the light of what has just been said, it would seem that the place for the local congregation to begin is in the study of the doctrine of the Church—that which really underlies its own existence. The study of the doctrine of the Church will lead both to a more vital congregational life on the local level and to a concern for Christian unity which is truly functional. Furthermore, a study of the doctrine of the Church will provide a framework in which the thorny problems of sacramental practice and ministerial succession can be placed in perspective and neither dismissed as irrelevant nor made into ends in themselves.

In several experiments for encouraging concern about Christian reunion on the local congregational level in which this writer has had a share, the first immediate result was a heightened interest in what one's own church really stood for. This has been true both in cases where the study groups were interdenominational and where they were from one communion or even one parish. An interest in the unique traditions of one's own denomination, however, can either make the whole project abortive or it can be the means through which the significance of the doctrine of the Church is appreciated for the first time.

This author writes as an Episcopalian who believes that he has a real appreciation for the heritage of his own communion in liturgical expression, sacramental life, and the historic succession of church order; and he is sure that the difference between his Church and other communions is often a difference in kind instead of a difference in degree. Yet this recognition and confession in no way denies what has just been said about the scandal and confusion caused by Christian divisions in those areas where they become clearest to see—in local congregational life. On the other hand, however, reference to this writer's own Anglican loyalties may serve to point a direction in which help may be found.

166

The major denominations in the world may have many similarities in practice, but each is the bearer of a tradition which was developed to meet the crying needs of people for the living gospel, and each has been enabled to minister to the lives of men and women in a truly creative way down through the centuries. The distinctive characteristics of the several major denominations are symbols of the kind of ministry that has been offered—which is not to say that something very similar may not have been provided by another group in a somewhat different way, nor is it to say that God uses only one kind of channel to bring his grace to human hearts.

The point may perhaps be illustrated by referring to the Book of Common Prayer as the normative expression of Episcopalian life—that which really provides for unity within congregations, which relates congregations to each other in spite of very different emphases on details, and which ties the ministry of the Church today to all that has gone before and to that which will come afterwards. The Book of Common Prayer is, therefore, the distinctive characteristic of Episcopalian life. While other churches have their service books which in many instances represent improvements on particular parts of the Book of Common Prayer, no other communion makes its service book serve quite the same purpose.

Other communions likewise have their own distinct treasures; the Presbyterians their concern for a dynamic presentation of the Bible as the Word of God and their tradition of lay ministerial character in the ruling eldership; the Methodists their emphasis on a religion of the heart as well as of the mind, and their concern for the practical expression of the fruits of the spirit; and the Congregationalists and Baptists, their insistence that individual freedom and true democracy belong not only in the political order but in the household of God. Each major tradition has its treasures of unique and distinct value.

If these distinctive characteristics and traditions are real treasures, this will not be just because they are described as such in books but rather because they are discovered to be such in congregational life. Therefore, it follows that to the extent that these things are real treasures of the Christian spirit, they must not be lost or even played down in order to achieve Christian reunion, for such a unity would only be an administrative coup, not a vic-

167

tory of the faith. Rather these treasures, particularly because they are appreciated so deeply in the local congregation, must be brought undamaged into the larger treasury of the united Church, and in this way what is achieved will be more truly representative of the Holy People of God.

Perhaps there is no better place in church life in which Christians of different traditions may make known to each other what their distinctive treasures are, and why these are valuable, than in a responsible kind of unity relationships between local congregations. Here the objective will not be to seize heaven by storm but to work out in the faith and life of living men and women whose loyalties ought to be real, what the meaning of the Christian Church is as a central aspect of the Christian faith.

Chapter Fifteen

Is There a Valid "Class" Heterogeneity in the Church?

Raymond M. Bost and Gaylord B. Noyce

Raymond M. Bost is minister to Lutheran Students at
Yale University; United Lutheran Church
Gaylord B. Noyce is pastor of the United Church, Ra-
leigh, N. C.; United Church of Christ

I. Social Stratification and the Church

The Church was called into being in a stratified society. The
community of the New Testament world was cut across by the
different social status accorded Jew as over against Greek, rich as
over against poor, learned as over against ignorant, free man as
over against slave, Greek as over against barbarian, male as over
against female. Throughout its history the Church has continued
to minister in a stratified society. While professing a unity that
transcends social differentiation, it has often seemed to belie its
profession by not only permitting social stratification to enter its
own life, but by actually contributing to this process. The movement of churches to suburbia, leaving the heterogeneity of the
inner city for a homogenized suburban location, is often cited as
the case in point. Those churches refusing to join the trek to
suburbia will often be found ministering not to the entire community surrounding their church edifice, but only to a certain segment of it. Even the congregation that does minister to differing
social segments in the community will often be found to have done
so at the cost of providing for social stratification within its own
life.

The liabilities in the warmth of a Protestant church fellowship which is built on the attraction of like for like have been pointed out by leading churchmen. Said Reinhold Niebuhr recently: "The churches, as Negro Christians long ago ruefully admitted, have been the most segregated communities in the South and, for that matter, in the nation. Nothing can hide the fact that this religiously sanctified racial parochialism has been a grievous offense against the very ideals of the Christian faith. But it has also been the negative by-product of one of the genuine achievements of the sectarian church in our nation; the creation of integral communities on the level of local congregations. Thus we have the ironic fact that the sports fields, theaters, and music halls of the nation have been more creative than the churches in establishing community between the races. This actual 'chumminess' of the local congregation has invalidated the universal principle at the heart of the gospel."[1]

As for the future, there are those who insist that the church of tomorrow will be called to minister in a society even more sharply divided into social classes than is our society of today. Whether this thesis be accepted or not, there is certainly little indication of an emerging classless society. Therefore the church must face the question squarely of how it can best discharge its mission in a stratified society. Can the church (i.e., congregation) best accomplish its mission by specializing in a ministry to only one segment of society, or can a congregation fulfill its task only through a ministry to all segments of the populace surrounding it?

II. Approaches to the Problem

Some, notably the Roman Catholics, have felt that social stratification should be largely ignored. Persons in a certain geographic area are enrolled as members in the church of that area. If a mission is started within the boundaries of a parish, persons near the mission are encouraged to attend Mass at the mission. If the mission develops into a parish, members from the older parish are transferred to the new one on the basis of their geographic location. While members of parish A may attend Mass in parish B, they remain members of Parish A and are expected to support it as their church.

---

[1]*The Reporter*, Nov. 29, 1956. Used by permission of Reinhold Niebuhr.

Many Protestants are quick to admit that they believe in the desirability of class churches. This is not just social snobbishness. The member of the middle-class group believes that the pentecostal mission is desirable because "It will reach a lot of people we could never get." Protestant groups may be found co-operating in the sponsorship of a rescue mission on the assumption that a more specialized ministry is needed for a particular group in the community than can be offered by existing churches. In the very processes of nature, specialization is manifest, and concomitant with specialization comes exclusiveness, even though exclusiveness may not be intended at all. Thus many congregations feel justified in gearing their ministry to one segment of the community, despite the geographical proximity of other social groups to the congregation in question.

A third pattern is also discernible. A congregation may minister to several segments of society by providing diverse worship, educational, and fellowship experiences. The liturgical church may provide a semiautonomous Sunday school. While the worship service of the church is quite formal and the hymns objective, the devotional period opening the Sunday school hour may, in effect, provide a brief nonliturgical service with subjective gospel hymns that would never be heard at the church service. A congregation may accomplish the same diversity in ministry through multiple services. The Sunday morning service may follow traditional liturgical forms, but the evening service be completely free of liturgical trappings. Organizations within the congregation may also by their distinctive emphasis contribute to the breadth of a congregation's ministry. While such a diverse congregational ministry may successfully attract people from various social strata, it does not always follow that the congregation has experienced true unity. It may merely have incorporated social differences into its own life. It would seem that most Protestants agree to the thesis that, human differences being what they are, the church must be willing to meet the specialized needs of people if its ministry is to be effective.

The fact that social stratification results in specialized religious needs is well demonstrated by H. Richard Niebuhr in *The Social Sources of Denominationalism*. The religion of the "disinherited" is distinctive because the needs of the group can be met only by an emotional, empirical religion. While the religious needs of the

171

middle class are not as easily defined as those of the proletariat, they are nevertheless distinct and, to a degree, discernible.

It is sometimes assumed that the very fact that cultural differences exist is the result of sin. Thus a diverse ministry on the part of the church might be regarded as contributing to the entrenchment of social evils. However, while it is easily recognized that sin contributes to social stratification, there is no reason to assume that members of the human race would all have had the same interests and capabilities if man had never sinned. Whether these innate differences and the resultant intellectual and economic differences would have been such as to justify a specialized ministry or not is open to question, but is nevertheless a factor to be considered before one places the label "SIN" on all cultural differences.

III. SPECIFIC ADVANTAGE FOR THE TYPES OF MINISTRY

A. In the light of current social stratification certain values can be suggested in ministering to a *homogeneous* segment of the community:

(1) *Evangelization:* The basic task of the Church is to proclaim the "good news" about God's decisive act in redeeming man. The proclamation of this message to a group of coal miners would have to be very different in form from the preaching of the same message to the faculty and students in a university chapel. By addressing himself to a homogeneous group the preacher can better communicate his message.

(2) *Education:* The church is called to teach. Both through pulpit and classroom, through curriculum-centered and pupil-centered teaching, communication is easier in a homogeneous group and hence there exists a larger possibility for Christian growth.

(3) *Worship:* Protestant worship requires that members of the congregation be participants rather than spectators. If the worshiping congregation is homogeneous, the worship service can be geared to its needs and result in larger participation in the service by the worshipers.

(4) *Fellowship:* There is ample biblical and sociological evidence to support the fact that man needs a sense of belonging. Where a congregation is composed primarily of those from the

same social class there is less embarrassment resulting from differences in dress, speech, and the like. Such differences create problems not only in connection with fellowship programs and banquets, but also in connection with regular church services, weddings, funerals, and so forth.

B. Some advantages in a congregation's ministering to a *heterogeneous group* are as follows:

(1) *Evangelization:* It is a basic part of the Church's gospel that a response of faith to the Church's proclamation results in the incorporation of the believer in the body of Christ, the one, holy, Catholic Church. Thus, practice and preaching seem more consistent when the congregation incorporates people from all social levels. Inclusiveness also enables a congregation to feel more readily its responsibility to minister to all levels of society rather than to a select group. It enables the church to make more manifest the fact that the only significant difference between men is in their relationship to Christ or lack of it.

(2) *Education:* The church can more easily teach its own inclusive nature if its inclusiveness is physical as well as spiritual, and it can recognize more clearly the legitimate breadth of its social responsibility.

(3) *Worship:* Some would maintain that a deeper sense of spirituality results from a manifestly heterogeneous group worshiping together. Many who worship in an interracial church sense a deeper spirituality in the worship. However, the novelty of the experience may account for this spiritual elevation or contribute to it. At least it can be said that a heterogeneous group points the participant to the true nature of worship, i.e., communion with God, rather than permitting him to find justification for church attendance in such superficialities as the mere mingling with a group of like-minded people.

(4) *Fellowship:* If the heterogeneous fellowship is to survive, it can do so only by leading its members to an appreciation of the inclusive nature of the church. Thus there is less danger of the fellowship within the congregation being non-Christian or even anti-Christian.

In attempting to weigh the advantages of a homogeneous congregation against those of a heterogeneous congregation a final question is raised: How important is a proper understanding of the inclusive nature of the church to the over-all ministry of the church? The advantages in a heterogeneous ministry center largely around an understanding of and a bearing witness to one aspect of the doctrine of the Church, namely its inclusiveness. Does the teaching of this point outweigh the values to be derived from a homogeneous ministry?

IV. SOME CONCLUSIONS FOR DEBATE

A. Clearly, one-class congregations will exist where there are one-class neighborhoods in American communities. These communities are produced by the draftsmanship of city planners and the changes of urban development. That a neighborhood church serving such a community tends to be a one-class church cannot be judged blameworthy. That the total program of such a church is geared to meet the needs of that community is only to be expected, for the greater effectiveness of the church's ministry. This church cannot be called exclusive if it repels a chance visitor merely because he prefers Bach and the choir sings Gounod, or because its minister wears no robe.

However, the assumptions in American culture which plan this type of community do need to be examined by the church. Serious thought needs to be given to the morality of city zoning and city planning which assign people their communities on the basis of income and race, and play a large role in molding American community life along a stratified pattern. Further, the strategy of the church extension executives needs to be questioned, for it results from many of the same assumptions held by the city planners. For example, given two sizable adjacent communities, one of the $20,000-home variety, one of the $12,000-, has a denomination any ministry of reconciliation to serve by planting one church at the juncture of the two communities rather than two churches, one in the middle of each tract?

B. Second, the "typing" of different churches will doubtless take place even within mixed communities. One church may work more with the disinherited, another with the intellectuals, and another with business groups, to whatever extent these stereotypes are valid and to whatever extent they represent determinative differences in the taste and the growing edge in the Christian understanding and experience of individuals. However, it seems to us

174

that in every one of these cases there must be a strong sense of contrition over the sin which contributes to these divisions. Some of the fruits of repentance are suggested below. If the church is to be a free expression of God's people gathering to express his praise in worship and in work, then such differences between them will occur. If we believed that there is but one divinely ordained form of polity and worship, then this should not occur, and a geographically divided parish arrangement should be a universal pattern. Our ecclesiology determines the norm we envision. Again, were the purpose of the church and its priesthood defined as a mere administration of the sacraments in the narrow sense, there would be no validity and actual sin manifest in the "typing" of churches in a heterogeneous community. We believe, however, that the varied functions implicit in Section III better embody the functions of the local congregation within the body of Christ in our culture.

We find little to indicate that the church needs to be divided along the lines of American denominationalism—as to say that it is logical that in community A there will be the Episcopalian, the Lutheran, the Presbyterian, and the Methodist type of belief if the heterogeneity of God's people is to be served most efficiently. We must admit that more of these divisions are caused by heritage— ethnic, family, or linguistic—than by individual choice of doctrine. Most denominations now encompass within them greater variety between their own extremes than as between the "median" of denomination A and denomination B; and most individual churches include wide differences of actual theological belief even in spite of a fairly definitive creedal and disciplinary norm to which the membership is expected to conform. Therefore it does not appear that "typing" by denominational label is as legitimate as it may have been at one time. This is not to say that human differences will not be reflected in different theological perspectives; it is to suggest that the denominational labels for these perspectives will not be determinative. From our experience, one community may have a "conservative" church with a Baptist affiliation and a "liberal" one with a Presbyterian tie; and the situation may be reversed in another community. Nor do we feel that ideally there is a heterogeneity in Christian doctrine. We simply deny that any one church will ever be entitled to recognition as the exclusive arbiter of what that doctrine is.

175

C. Third, one of the courses of action which follow these observations adds an "Amen" to efforts at ecumenicity. The catholicity of the church and the advantages of heterogeneity within the experience of a churchman are important enough to suggest that the local congregation needs a genuine experience of the inclusiveness of the Holy Catholic Church. If by reason of neighborhood, or by reason of increased effectiveness in its mission and the meaning of its worship, the congregation appears to have a valid class orientation, a balance for this limitation must be found in a more vital connectionalism in the interchurch dimension. The congregation needs a strong sense of the fact that it belongs to a fellowship, a church, which in actuality does transcend the lines of status and taste, of caste and class. This can be true within the denominations, since the denomination may include the across-the-tracks, the rural, and the urban church. The strengthening of denominational unity by the elimination of racially determined denominational units is a case in point. Beyond that, the increased vitality of the conciliar movement would be indicated, for there is still some validity in rough generalizations about the class orientation of the denominations.

One metaphor which may be useful to describe our goal is that of the "parish-cathedral" experience. While the parish, or the local congregation, may perforce be "typed," there must be within its experience its identity with the transcendent Church, still institutional and on earth though it be, which embraces all segments of society. Within the large multi-class church the analogy holds as well. Some advantage may accrue from having these varied class groups (the men's Bible class, the Sunday school, the prayer meeting) meeting under the same roof while still stratified; but this type of church will not necessarily realize the inclusive nature of the church because of the strength of cultural ties. The church must have a definite strategy and program to bring its members to a realization of their unity in Christ.

D. Again, it would be expected that this perspective be reflected in the educational and worship experience of the local congregation. Church school materials and teacher training must present the unity of the Church above race and class divisions. The historical sources of the divisions of the Church may be presented for an understanding of them; the denigration of other class or denominational churches should cease. The unity of the Church in the theological sense must take its place alongside other teaching.

Again, in the use of worship materials, the use of the great body of liturgical material and the great hymns and music from the historical Christian tradition will be used more and more even if there is no universally prescribed liturgical norm. These materials will cross denominational and class lines, and tend to eliminate some of the more extreme parochialism of class worship.

E. One of the valid goals of socio-economic organization for most believers in democracy is a maximum social mobility which works for the greatest individual fulfillment in life. So, too, we believe, for the church. If we acquiesce to the probability of some church "typing," at the same time we insist on the openness of the whole structure. There must be a genuine welcome on the part of any church for that person from outside who finds himself interested in its particular form of worship, teaching, or activity. Here is the test of the reality of inclusiveness, if there is more than a "front-room" welcome for the stranger within the gates. The absence of this welcome is the great sin of the church's disunity, rather than the simple fact that various churches express their life in differing forms which tend by their nature to attract persons from one class.

V. Summary

The Church is an article of faith. We *believe* in the Holy, Catholic Church. Should we insist that the inclusiveness of the Church must be physically proved in the crucible of every congregation's life, would we not be in danger of accepting the position (held in Rome) that the only real unity in the Church is that which is manifest before the eyes of the world? Can we truly *believe* in the Church in the same way we believe in God the Father and in his Son Jesus Christ, and at the same time demand a visible, material manifestation of the Church in the life of each congregation?

The whole question we are given may need amendment. The unity we seek? It must be stated first that we are given a unity in Christ. The unity we seek is a proper realization of that given unity, a realization in the Church of the world and in the local congregation. We live, therefore, confessing the degree to which worldly disunity has kept us from this realization and kept us from manifesting it to the world.

The deeper the realization of the unity that is already given in Christ, the more clearly this unity will be manifest to the world through co-operative endeavors and public acceptance of one another as Christians, and even in the organizational structure of the churches. Such a growth in the realization of our unity need not abridge the freedom we have in Christ and the effectiveness of the churches' mission to a stratified society. This most certainly means an end to exclusiveness in attitudes, but we cannot say it means the enforcement of a unity in worship or polity or doctrine on some "least-common-denominator" basis. To say it did would be a denial of the unity we already have; it would imply that there is no unity until we ourselves build it. Our unity must come from obedience to our given unity in Christ, rather than from a defensive attempt to impress the world with our efficiency or power or prestige. The vision of one Holy Catholic Church is our faith, our already realized faith in the worship of Him who is her foundation.

Chapter Sixteen

Caste and Class in the Local Church

Warren Ashby

Associate Professor of Philosophy at the Woman's College
of the University of North Carolina; Methodist Church

The Christian Church in theory is an inclusive fellowship in which there is "neither Jew nor Greek, there is neither bond nor free, there is neither male nor female." The Christian churches, in actuality, are exclusive organizations with restrictive covenant clauses. The most obvious exclusiveness in the local Protestant churches in the United States is racial and economic:

(1) "Less than 1 per cent of the white congregations have any Negro members (and each of these generally has only two or three), and less than one-half of 1 per cent of the Negro Protestants who belong to 'white denominations' worship regularly with white persons. (Less than 8% of Negro Protestants belong to "white denominations.")

(2) "Individual Protestant churches tend to be 'class churches,' with membership drawn principally from one class group. Even where membership cuts across class lines, control of the church and its policies is generally in the hands of officials drawn from one class, usually the middle class."[1]

Here, then, are clear symptoms of disease in the Church. Before there can be cure, there should be diagnoses to discover the causes of the symptoms, and to find whether the symptoms are the disease or but ways in which a deeper dis-ease manifests itself.

From the many ways a diagnosis can take place the approach to be used here is to analyze the functions of the local church and the implicit attitudes which the members, clergy, and laity, take toward their church. We will not be dealing with institutional statements

[1]Pope, Liston, "Religion and the Class Structure, in *Annals of the American Academy of Political and Social Science,* vol. 256, March, 1948, pp. 89-91.

of belief regarding the church as these appear in theology or ritual. We will not be concerned with the explicitly stated attitudes of the members. Nor in the analysis will we be making value judgments; the initial purpose is to understand the functionings of the church, not to condemn or approve.

The analysis begins with the recognition that the church, as an institution, and church members possess an "institutional environment" that has interrelations with the functionings and the members' understandings of the local church. "When we speak of the institutional environment, we mean the various customary ways in which people think and act when they pursue their principal roles and attempt to maintain their key status in the social structure."[2] Church members are obviously more than church members. They are involved in society in many ways and in many institutions. (Or, according to the jargon, individuals "pursue roles.") They "rock 'n roll" from institution to institution as individuals, always carrying with them something of the outlook, the ways of thinking and acting which they have experienced in a particular involvement or institution. Therefore it is possible to develop correlations between the functionings of the nonreligious and the religious institutions, and between the individual's attitudes in his nonchurch experiences as these relate to his church life. Sometimes the correlations are casual; sometimes they exist because the experiences in the separate institutions arise from similar causes outside both. In either case, the relations may be suggestive for understanding the racial and economic exclusiveness of the local church.

What are some of the involvements of the church member in modern society? What are the nonreligious institutions in which he plays a significant role? (1) The church member, obviously, is also a member of an American family which, as an institution, is still in process of profound changes. (2) He is involved, directly or indirectly, in "making a living"; and in the present American economic system is, therefore, part of a "business enterprise." (3) The church person is a participant in a social group that, taking many forms, appears most clearly in his place of residence and membership in social clubs. (4) The citizens of the kingdom are also citizens of a nation-state that has become increasingly dominant in the lives of American people. (5) Most of the persons in a

[2]Fichter, Joseph H., *Social Relations in the Urban Parish*, University of Chicago Press, 1954, pp. 108-109. Used by permission.

church have some relation to the public school, a relation that has a great influence in their lives. (6) Thus far church members have been noted as participants in other institutions. But they are inescapably involved in the mid-twentieth century United States; this is to say, they are users of the technology, in particular, consumers of the mass media. From the manipulation of machines and the hound of television there seems to be no escape. (7) All church members are related to these institutions. But there is another institution, religious yet nonlocal church, in which the "professional Christians" participate. These persons, formally educated in religion, have become such an important part of the Protestant church that their special situation must be recognized. This is the institution of "the Ecumenical movement" and these are sometimes called facetiously the "Ecumaniacs."

Now what are the functions of these institutions and what kind of experiences do church members have within them? How are such functions and experiences correlated with the functionings of and attitudes toward the local church? We shall, in the analysis, give special attention to the first three and only passing notice to the latter four involvements.

I. The Church as Contemporary American Family

The family system in the United States has, throughout the current century, been undergoing profound transformations; and since the local church consists of persons who have experienced and are experiencing within the family these changes, the church is inevitably characterized by some of the elements of the contemporary American family.

Many observers have noted dominant motifs of the new "nuclear family" of which the following is typical:

> The basic and irreducible functions of the family are two: first, the primary socialization of the children so they can truly become members of the society into which they have been born; second, the stabilization of the adult personalities of the population of the society.[3]

In the process of socialization the family enables its members to function in other institutions; but the point is that in the other institutions they function as individuals and not as members of

[3]Parsons, Talcott and Bales, Robert F., *Family, Socialization and Interaction Process,* Free Press, 1955, p. 16. Used by permission.

the family. And the family provides a stability for its members; but it is a stability that primarily enables individuals to endure the instabilities of society rather than to introduce order into the society. The relations within the family, then, are contractual and democratic. There is an emphasis upon individualism rather than a concern for the family as such. Again, the nuclear family is a relatively independent unit, independent from both kin and community. The family is centered upon the immediate members; created by marriage, the modern family most often has separate residence for the immediate family members, and it lasts only so long as it performs satisfactorily one or both of its basic functions. The family, thus, is not a kinship or an inclusive community group, it does not have economic or even formal educational or religious functions, it is not permanent in place or time, it does not have binding to a larger family or to the land.

Now many of these same characteristics are evident in the local church. A. The church is primarily nuclear, centering upon its individual members. It is thus independent from its past and from its society. To a large extent the local church is even independent from its "kin"; indeed many local churches would have difficulty identifying the "kindred minds." This autonomy is true despite the fact that organizational structures (denominations, councils) seem to be steadily tightening. Indeed there may be a relation between the loss of kinship and the increasing organization.

B. The local church, like the nuclear family, is contractual in nature, with a real impermanence in time and place. Thus there is lack of loyalty to the local institution despite the fact that the local church is becoming increasingly institutionalized. But institutionalism is not the result of loyalty to an institution, i.e., to its inner meaning and purposes. Institutionalism is, in fact, faithlessness to the institution. Moreover the church, like the family, is impermanent in time and place. In no country, in no time, have individuals been able to move so casually from one "totem" to another, from one "cathedral" to another. And the familiar sight of a church being moved bodily from place to place is also unique. After the Christians rose in the world from the catacombs they did not move the downtown church from Rome to the suburbs.

C. Again, the church through structure, ritual, and preaching is directed toward giving stability to the lives of its adults in an unstable society. This is done overtly through the preaching and teaching of the church. The most prominent forms of Protestant Christianity make the Christian faith a success story, either in this life or the next, with little emphasis upon unlimited religious or ethical demands.

D. The local church, again like the nuclear family, has as one of its primary functions the "socialization" of its members. Through use of popular and accepted social methods the church enables the individual to function more effectively in other institutions; but he functions in those other institutions as an individual and not as a member of the church.

II. The Local Church as Business Enterprise

The members of the church are directly involved in making a living; and this means that they have roles to play as part of some business enterprise with stakes in the success of the "business." Because of the power of the business institution and mind in contemporary society, it would, indeed, be strange if all the institutions of society, including the church, did not share some of the characteristics of a business enterprise.

The dominant and ultimate drive of any business is the desire for profit, for a profit that is measurable on the books and in the banks; and this means that the business exists first of all to satisfy its stockholders and owners. To make a profit, a business is organized in personnel and work. In personnel there is a hierarchy and division of authority and responsibility; in work there is allocation of necessary functions. In the organization there is, by and large, co-operation within the business and competition without. Sales exist as an essential part of the business and the sales may be made in a variety of ways: by improving the product, by meeting the needs of customers, by increasing the needs of the customers, and by persuading the customers that they have needs they didn't know existed. Two other factors regarding modern business should be noted; and both seem to have strong analogues with the local church. One is that the business is dependent upon an accounting system that provides essential information for the

183

decision-making boys. The nature of this information is important:

One of the main functions of the hierarchy is to prevent information from reaching its upper ranks except in highly abstract and condensed form. . . . The top executives must be spared the knowledge that machine X in shop Y needs oiling or that customer Z is dissatisfied with his purchase and returned it.[4]

Finally, a business organization becomes a continuing organism that struggles to survive, and this struggle is independent of the particular members who give it birth. Every business has a vested interest in its own continued existence.

Turning to the local church, it is obvious that it possesses many of these same characteristics and that it can, indeed, be viewed as a "business." The business entity of the church is ambiguous. Sometimes the local church is but a part of a larger business (the denomination); sometimes it is an independent small business.

A. The local church is an organism that struggles to survive and that is independent of the particular persons who initiated the church. The church, in keeping with the "drive to survive" theory of institutions, has a nisus for existence. If churches are born through pain and travail, they seem to die even harder.

B. The church also possesses an intricate organization of personnel and of work. At times it may appear questionable whether in the local church, as in business, there is co-operation within the organization and competition without; but in general this is true. In the organization there is an intricate accounting system usually devised by the denominational hierarchy, usually accepted by the local lower-archy. Of the making of reports there seems to be no end. The nature of the information in church reports as in business accounting seems to have a similar characteristic, viz., to communicate information in an abstract, impersonal form so that the "top ecclesiastical executives" will be spared the news that teacher X in department Y needs oiling, or that Christian Z has become dissatisfied with his purchase. There is one apparent difference between church and business accounting: business accounting has the purpose of communicating information in order

---

[4]Boulding, Kenneth, *The Organizational Revolution,* Harper and Brothers, 1935, p. 135. Used by permission.

that persons in responsible positions might make informed decisions.

C. The local church is also concerned with "sales" of belief or activity or status which the church has to offer. These sales may be made by improving the product, by meeting the needs of the customers, by increasing the needs of the customers, and by persuading the customers that they have needs they didn't know existed.

D. The local church is also interested in "making a profit" that is measurable. The profit is thought of most frequently in terms of a "growing church," that is, growing in members and in finances. Growing in grace is not easily measured.

E. Finally, the local church exists to satisfy the customers, the members of the organization, and the stockholders and owners; and in a church these are generally the same persons. But just as in a business the satisfaction of the owner takes primacy over the other two groups, it often appears that in a local church the stockholder or owner attitude is basic. If the "profit" is not adequate, the stockholders can change the management ("we need a younger man, Bishop") or demand different products ("less ritual," "more Bible in church school lessons").

III. The Local Church as Social Club

The members of the local church associate primarily with persons of similar social and economic status. These status-relations reflected in the residences of church members are manifest even more clearly in the kinds of voluntary social associations in which individuals participate. A St. Paul traveling in the United States from town to town would no longer be greeted with a sign from the apostles but by a sign of Kiwanians, the Business Professional Women, the Garden Clubbers, to say nothing of the Elks, the Moose, the Lions, the International Woodmen of the World, and their Auxiliaries.

Americans could not, of course, be a race of club-hoppers unless the organizations served human needs and satisfied human interests. What are some of these needs and interests that social clubs meet? First, obviously, is the need for social fellowship. Human beings desire to share life, to enjoy life with other like-minded persons with whom they are at ease. It may be that this is a need for like-unminded persons; for social clubs place a minimum of intellectual demands upon their members. There is also the need for emotional release that is met through club participation; and it may be that many a man who can no longer sound "Amen!" in the church with propriety is able, in a hotel, to roar like a Lion. Society organizations also provide opportunities for sharing viewpoints. Persons who are fond of Nixon or the United Nations or camellias need the experience of confirming with others the essential soundness and wisdom and morality of their views. The clubs also possess an exclusiveness and thus enhance the members' desire for status. Sometimes the entrance requirements are class or economic; sometimes they are caste or racial; sometimes they are professional or hobby. Invariably the entrance requirements of a social club are external and not in terms of what a person essentially is but what he possesses. It may take money but it does not take virtue to be a member of the country club; it may take status but it doesn't require special intelligence to be a Rotarian; it may take religious affiliation but it doesn't take much faith to be a Knight of Columbus or a Mason. The clubs also have a humanitarian interest. There is present in almost every social club a genuine interest in service. They are designed to promote world-understanding, or Americanism, or a more beautiful city. But in no case is humanitarianism the dominant purpose of the social club. Those primary purposes are fellowship and status.

Now many of these same characteristics are present within the local church. A. Humanitarianism is present in the local church. Indeed the commandment to love would seem to make a religious oriented humanitarianism one *raison d'être* of the local church. But an examination of the budget of money or time will gave some rough indication of the extent of Christocentric humanitarianism. Does the local church and do its members really want to help others in terms of unique personal needs or are the concerns to help others in superficial standard ways? The remark of the social caseworker about her profession may be true for many churchmen: "We're here to help others; but what the others are here for God only knows."

B. The entrance requirements of the church, like those of a social club, are primarily external and they provide status. Like club-folk the church-folk are kind, genteel, inoffensive. Thus the entrance requirements, often stated in outworn phraseology of an earlier era, are usually interpreted to possess a generality of meaning. The requirements are external in that one must profess a faith before men; but this does not necessarily mean that the profession has substance in fact as well as in words. And, again like the social club, once the entrance requirements for admission are passed, the requirements for remaining within the church are not difficult to meet. It is not hard to be a Rotarian. Nor is it difficult to be a member of a local church.

C. There is in the local church, as in a social club, a sharing of viewpoints and a minimum of intellectual demands. The viewpoints shared are usually those acceptable in the community-at-large. At least the ideas most frequently expressed within the church are not designed to disturb the social or religious order. The minimum of intellectual demands refers to the fact that doubting, the asking of embarrassing intellectual questions, is not fashionable within the church. The idea is somehow conveyed to large numbers of young intellectuals that since doubting represents a lack of faith, it is sinful and therefore like other sins is to be suppressed or at least not practiced openly. As a recent visitor to one university put it: "If you go to college for four years and never ask searching religious questions or are never plagued by religious doubts, you haven't been to college. You've been to church."

D. Within the church as within the social club there is opportunity for emotional release. Some of this release occurs in the normal expenditure of energy, in engagement in activities, in being associated with other persons. More of the release in church, though, occurs within the setting of worship; and here the church provides what a social club with its quasi-religious tones often suggests but can never offer directly, viz., a religious signification for the emotional release. Sometimes in the church the emotion takes on a profound personal meaning. This deeper experience may come during a special religious celebration; or it may come with the shock of death, of sickness, of helplessness; or at times with the shock of success. At such times a social club may attempt to provide a substitute for the genuinely religious emotion; but it is necessarily a weak substitute.

187

E. The greatest similarity of the social club and the church in both the church's functioning and in the attitudes of its members exists in that large area of experience termed "social fellowship." Here is the strength of the club in that it provides for human beings: (1) a warmth of companionship, (2) a sense of belonging to others and with others, and (3) a cause the self feels worth serving. The local church in its worship, its church school, its extra meetings and activities provides all of these "social fellowship" values. Yet the quality of the companionship, the community, and the cause should be carefully examined. A social club offers a warmth of companionship without touching the real springs of a person's life or behavior. This may also be true of the local church; for persons separated from each other by the nature of modern living are not likely to penetrate to each other's real self either at a club dinner or with a handshake-and-so-long after the morning worship. Moreover, while a club offers companionship, it is relatively impersonal. In the hotel lobbies throughout the country the visiting Lion is cordially greeted and his name is pinned to his lapel; but the name on the lapel represents more of a label than a person. Is it any different for a visitor to a church on a Sunday morning? Does the very companionship of a church, as of a club, tend to obscure a dominant fact of our time: that persons are separated from persons?

Again, within the church as within the club there is a sense of belonging to others and with others. But what is the quality of this belongingness? Is it the quality expressed recently by a North Carolina church member: "Parson, we didn't go to see that fellow you said was having a tough time because after we talked it over, we were not certain he was the kind of person we wanted in our church." Is there conveyed in our local churches that simple sense of belonging to others who, at times, are all but overcome by the trivia and the power of life and death. In Greensboro recently a four-year-old boy and a five-year-old girl found some candy and ate it. The candy was digitalis. Within twelve hours the boy was dead; within twenty-four hours the girl, too, died. There is no doubt that neighbors, that friends of the families, felt through this tragedy a new sense of belonging to each other. But was that simple deep relation felt in any unique way by the members of the churches to which the families belonged?

Finally, a social club provides a cause, a goal. To be sure, the cause is temporary, the goal is ephemeral. But this fact is either not recognized (as with those who make a religion of the DAR, their labor union, or the Junior Chamber of Commerce), or it is conveniently forgotten for the time being. The church, too, provides a cause. But often that cause seems just as ephemeral, just as temporary, as those of the social clubs. The youth of the church are asked if they want to give their lives to Christ. When, with that abandon, that selflessness characteristic of many youths, they answer "yes," what realistic causes are they asked to serve? To raise their hand, to sign a pledge, to attend the youth fellowship, and—it may be—to "enter full-time Christian service." The adult in the church is urged to make Christ real in his everyday life. And when he turns a half-inquiring mind and heart asking what specifically this means, he too often receives the same musty answers ("Pray and have faith") that do not help him to focus upon the urgent, the real problem of his work and life.

This analysis of the Church as Family and as Business and as Club Ecclesia may be sufficient to indicate one line of inquiry that might be fruitful for understanding the divisions within the church. But further inquiry is required to explain other aspects of the institutional environment. Further analyses should include: (A) the involvement of the individual and the church in the nation-state that is known in terms of impersonality, and power, and demands, and welfare; (B) the church members' experience of mass communications, pre-eminently in coming years with the consumption of television programs and emphases of being entertained, the passive acceptance or passive rejection of what is presented, the sedation of thought and moral action, the learning about the world from a limited, armchair perspective; (C) the relations of the church clientele to the public schools with the professionalization of education, the day-care of children, the non-participating of the parent in the educating process, social promotions; and (D) the ecumenical experiences of Christians with emphases upon common beliefs and organizations.

IV. Contemporary Society and Exclusiveness in the Church

Each of these analyses taken separately provides interesting clues for specific understandings of the church. Since race and

189

economic divisions cut through most of the institutions, the analyses taken separately provide particular insights for comprehending caste and class within the church. Added together the clues provide a massive portrayal of contemporary American society that has a direct effect upon the church. *Some* of these characteristics are: (A) the scope of change, (B) the organizational revolution, (C) the fragmentation of life, and (D) impersonal and social relations.

A. *The scope of change* refers to the fact that "whirl is king."

> One thing that is new is the prevalence of newness, the changing scale and scope of change itself, so that the world alters as we walk in it, so that the years of a man's life measure not some small growth or re-arrangement or moderation of what he learned in childhood, but a great upheaval.[5]

Failure to grasp this fact adequately means that our institutions, the local church in particular, try to solve now problems with formulae that were devised for old and past situations.

B. *The organizational revolution* (a term originated by the economist, Kenneth Boulding) refers to one of the leading motifs of our changing society.

> One aspect of the many-sided revolution through which we have been passing is the "organizational revolution." . . . It has crept upon us silently. . . . In our political and economic thinking, and in our ethical thinking as well, we are still often a hundred years behind the times—still thinking of a society in which organizations are rather small and weak.[6]

This organizational revolution, this institutionalizing of life, is having a profound impact on the life of the local church in general and upon the divisions within the Church in particular.

C. *The fragmentation of life* is the culmination of an historical process that may have special interest and relevance for the Protestant churches since an initial impetus for this fragmentation was provided by the Protestant Reformation. The separateness of the parts of life, the specialization of the functions of life, have become characteristic; and the most obvious attempts in our time to overcome the fragmentation have either been abortive or have led to a greater disorder than the shattered fragments.

---

[5]J. Robert Oppenheimer, in "Columbia Bicentennial Lecture," reprinted in *Arts and Architecture*, January, 1955, p. 4. Used by permission.
[6]Boulding, *op. cit.*, p. 4.

D. *The impersonal and societal relations* refer to what is both a characteristic and a consequence of change, of the organizational revolution, of the fragmentation of life. The relations of the self are impersonal and societal rather than personal and community relations. And this refers to the self dwelling with institutions, with things, with nature, with art, with other individuals, and with the self. It refers, too, to the Ultimate relations of the individual. This also has tended to become impersonal and societal. Further marks of this impersonality and sociality of life means that the current emphases are more in terms of: (1) socialization of individuals and not nonconformity of persons; (2) superficial mass emotions and not the unique depths of personal life; (3) program entertainment and "spectator sports" rather than participation and involvement; (4) contractual relations that are temporary and not binding covenants (with others, with the community, with God); (5) individual profit and welfare rather than commitment, sacrifice, discipline, service; (6) "second-hand experiences" and not primary study, thought, creations; (7) symbols as jargon rather than being grasped by a new truth, a new and living Word.

But what has all this to do with the problems with which we began, in the problems of class and caste divisions in the church? Those divisions, the exclusiveness of the local church, are a part of the total picture. In some ways the caste and class exclusiveness are characteristic of the impersonal and societal relations. In other ways they may be viewed as a result of and as cutting through all the characteristics of our time. In either case the disorder is pervasive and powerful. To comprehend its permeating quality and its force, the disorder in the local church must be understood in its full personal and institutional setting. The analysis of the institutional environment may provide some clues to the disorder and some possibilities for transformations. But other approaches, obviously, are also needed.

This examination of the institutional environment of the local church has been an attempt to be objective and analytical. Such attempts are essential. In 1911 before the *first* World War, Ernst Troeltsch wrote:

> If the present social situation is to be controlled by Christian principles, thoughts will be necessary which have not yet been thought, and which will correspond to this new situation as the older forms met the need of the

social situation in earlier ages. These ideas will have to be evolved out of the inner impulse of Christian thought, and out of its vital expression at the present time.[7]

If this is to happen, there must be an understanding of the "new situation"; and this comes in part through objective analysis. But there must be more than analysis; and there are grave perils in such analysis.

There is the danger, first, that too much analysis may prevent the analysts from doing what is required, what is essential here and now. The greater peril is that analysis may give us a false sense of objectivity, an erroneous sense that we are looking at others, that we are dealing with what is happening to others, that cures can be made by giving prescriptions for others. But *we* are involved. *We* live in this total society and, as Richard Niebuhr points out, this society lives in us. Let us know, then, that there is exclusiveness in the church, that there are caste and class divisions here. Let us know more: that we are in the church and of the church; and that in a very real way—perhaps in an inescapable way—this exclusiveness, this divisiveness, this disorder is in us. Let us analyze and prescribe. But the fundamental problems are not impersonal, objective questions: what shall be done in the institution? The basic question about disease in the church is a simple question because it is personal: "Wilt thou be made whole?"

[7]Troeltsch, Ernst, *Social Teachings of the Christian Churches*, 1931, vol. 2, p. 1012.

Chapter Seventeen

Sacrifices and Disciplines in a Local Church

Seido Ogawa

Pastor of the Community Church, Waipahu, Oahu, T. H.; Congregational-Christian Churches (now the United Church of Christ)

Membership in any organization assumes a measure of discipline. To a certain degree it is assumed that the well-being of the group and the purpose for which it exists are matters of shared concern. The minimal discipline which individual members are expected to accept is that the interests and desires of the group be recognized and given consideration alongside of, and sometimes even in opposition to, more personal interests and desires. Any organization has a legitimate claim upon a measure of a member's time, thought, and talent. Not to recognize this is to erase, in effect, the membership status of the person. To the degree that the constituent members of an organization allow the purpose, program, and functions of the group to dictate their use of their time and energy for ends which are recognized to be in the interests of the group as a whole, as against more personal interests, to that degree an organization disciplines its individual members.

The church shares this general type of relationship between organization and members. To the degree that any local church wins the commitment of its members to its purpose and mission, and to the life it leads, so that the effectiveness and vitality of the church's life is a matter of some real concern to those mem-

193

bers, to that degree the church and what it stands for exercises a discipline over its members. That discipline is the basis of unity in a church as in other organizations.

But there is a difference between a church and other organizations in the nature and degree of the commitment it seeks and evokes. It is a matter of fact and experience that in general the Church has succeeded through the years in enlisting greater, more unreserved commitment from its members than is true of other organizations. The discipline which the Church has been able to exercise over its members has been on the whole more deep-rooted and lasting than is true in other organizations. The unity of a local church is more deepseated and continuing, and less likely to be broken completely. And the discipline of the church upon its members' lives tends, on the whole, to be a more total discipline—over the whole individual—rather than the more specific and limited types of discipline that pertains to membership in other groups.

These differences are rooted in the one fundamental difference between a church and any other organization. Every other organization tends, in a sense, to be an end in itself. The commitment which it seeks from its members, and the discipline it seeks to impose on its members, is for the sake of strengthening and glorifying itself. The most altruistic aims and stated purposes do not really give it an orientation and end beyond itself. On the other hand, the Church, by its very nature and by what it stands for in the understanding of people (to a greater degree than we usually realize) is far larger than itself. The commitment which it seeks from people, and the discipline it seeks to impose, is not for the sake of its own glorification, but to the end that the Almighty God shall be enthroned and the mission of its Lord Jesus Christ shall be fulfilled. In a basic sense, and to a degree never quite as genuine with any other organization, the church's discipline (sought and attained) over its members is not oriented to its own satisfaction but to the satisfaction of a mission which is more than itself.

To put it another way, other organizations discipline their members but themselves are not subject to a higher discipline. On the other hand the church is always, at a basic level of its consciousness, aware of itself as subject in turn to the will of God as that will is set forth in the life and ministry of Christ.

194

Other organizations can seek the co-operation of their members to further the interests of the group as a whole, but they do not point with the same persistency or underlying consciousness to a purpose and ultimate goal that is clearly beyond the life of the group. The church not only disciplines its members but is itself continually under the discipline of the mission which it has been given to discharge.

The recognition that we are primarily and fundamentally joined together in a local church, as a means to an end that transcends the church itself, constitutes a very basic kind of discipline and unity that is distinctive to the nature and being of a church. It tends to evoke a kind of unified and unqualified response of the whole individual that in turn makes for a fundamental unity between individual members, a unity that, in a real sense, stems from the oneness of God rather than any desire for unity on man's part.

The question is: To what degree, in what sense, can this discipline that makes for unity in the local church also be a basis of increasing unity among churches? Certain facts become obvious. The local church, the denominations, must fight the encroachment of institutionalism—the tendency to make itself an end rather than a means. What church or denomination would be willing to claim itself as an end and not a means? And yet it is this very tendency toward institutionalism that creates a growing number of churches of Christ rather than the one Church in many parts. If a church or denomination can persistently and courageously and sacrificially distinguish between the tendency to satisfy and save its own life and the losing of that life for the sake of the Gospel, the most fundamental cause of disunity among churches would be wiped out. If churches and denominations would accept the same discipline they seek to impose upon their members, of orientation to the ultimate Christian task, they would possess the unity which, in Christ, is inescapable. But when they pervert the means to an end, they not only encourage disunity, but falsify the basis upon which they seek discipline over people's lives. Within the Christian movement the central teaching of Jesus is just as applicable to churches as to individuals, that "he who seeks to save his life shall lose it." And institutionalism is a sure mark of self-centeredness and the loss of the only kind of vitality the Gospel offers.

195

If correct Christian discipline is applied to churches as well as to individuals, it would be rather impossible for any church to claim superiority over any other, because in itself, it would be nothing. It would have validity and vitality only in relation to the greater mission of the Church universal to preach the Gospel to mankind.

We would say of churches what Paul says in 1 Corinthians 3: What then are Baptists, what are Episcopalians, or Methodists, but historical expressions of man's response to the call of God? One may plant and another water and another reap, but it is God who gives life and increase. Apart from that life and vitality which God offers alike to all, we are nothing. We are therefore called to be laborers together in God's vineyard, and our reward shall surely come from God and not from men.

By clearly establishing the fact that the Church on earth is always a means to the end, we would move from the tendency to glorify and fortify the Church's life to a more certain absorption with the business of the Church which is to preach Christ and him crucified. We would be seeking unity not by the method of patchwork, that is, by fitting together clearly identifiable and self-conscious entities, but by losing ourselves, our individual selves and our church selves, in the cause of the Gospel.

By allowing institutionalism to take hold of us the Church is betraying its own members, who, even though they may not be clearly aware of the basis of their commitment, are not really committed to their own church or denomination but to the Christian Gospel as a universal fact. We are taking advantage of the closeness of the local church to the local member, and the natural loyalties that pertain to this relationship, and failing to nourish the deeper yearning of mind and soul after a more unified and integrated life which is the underlying basis of their commitment.

The unity we seek, the only unity that we can have, is one that individual differences cannot destroy. There is only one basis of such a unity, and that is to render our differences as churches or as individuals less decisive than the commonness of our need and our mission. This is not possible unless and until churches can accept the discipline of common enlistment in a cause that transcends the capacities, and the very understanding, of men and churches—a cause that, in the end, will have to be brought to fruition, not by the accomplishment of men, but by the grace of God.

Chapter Eighteen

The Theological Implications of Mobility

Yoshio Fukuyama

Director of Department of Research, Board of Home Missions, Congregational-Christian Churches (now United Church of Christ)

Truman B. Douglass recently observed that something is happening in the life of the Church in our time as momentous as any reformation in the history of the Church. He asserted that "theological work and biblical study are being carried on with a range and penetration not matched since the sixteenth century." He pointed to this work of "thinking in wider company" as possessing a peculiar urgency for us in America and that it ultimately means asking in a new and urgent way the central questions about the nature of the church and its mission.[1] Our Study Conference at Oberlin is an important aspect of this new reformation.

This paper is written not by one fluent in the discourse of ecumenical theology. Rather, it is written by one whose professional orientation is the sociology of religion, whose work is in the area of descriptive sociological analysis rather than normative theological principles. But for sociologists who are also churchmen, there is the inevitable convergence of theology with sociology, the necessity of interpreting sociological data in the context of the Christian faith.

---

[1] *Preaching and the New Reformation*, New York: Harper & Brothers, 1956.

One axiom which has always been implicit when a sociologist thinks theologically is that, generally speaking, the content of any theological norm can be gauged by the demand it makes on social organization. The term "fellowship," for example, may be understood theologically as referring to the *koinōnia of* the early church, the togetherness of the Christian community and its acts of mutual sharing and worship. In biblical parlance it is the third dimension of "the Grace of the Lord Jesus Christ and the Love of God." But the same term can be devoid of all theological content when the reference is simply to "food and fun."

So it is with these thoughts in mind that we address ourselves to a consideration of the theological implications of mobility in American life. It is hoped that this preliminary attempt to raise some theological questions will provide a starting point for the emergence of the kind of theological undergirding required for our co-operative Christian ministries to America on the move. This undergirding is imperative if these ministries are to be marked by spiritual penetration and faithfulness to our common Christian mission to America.

Daniel T. Jenkins once proposed a tent as the ideal prototype for a church building. A tent suggests a building for people on the march, a mobile congregation, ready to move on to new frontiers. In the context of Judeo-Christian history, the suggestion is not fanciful. The history of the Hebrew Commonwealth was one couched in the mobility of peoples. Joseph and Mary, we are reminded, had to return from Galilee to Judea to be counted in the imperial census. The New Testament record of the first century of the Church makes frequent references to "strangers and sojourners," to the need to "show hospitality to strangers," and Paul's letters bridge the spatial distance traveled by early Christian witnesses as the Church began to take a foothold in the far-flung Roman Empire.

Indeed, the history of the expansion of Christianity over twenty centuries has been the history of human mobility. The fundamental theological problem, therefore, is a perennial one: it is that of the relationship of Christ to culture.

Sociologically, mobility implies exposure to new places, new ideas, and the emergence of new cultural patterns. It may disorganize habits, unsettle routines, break up customs, and undermine faiths. Mobility may also be an occasion for broadening perspectives, for reassessing long-accepted practices and deepening understanding and faith.

H. Richard Niebuhr's well-known study of this "enduring theological problem" identifies five ways in which the Church has, through the ages, sought to meet the problems posed by culture.[2] These types include (1) "Christ against culture" which is exemplified in the Mennonite rejection of political participation and military service; (2) "Christ of culture" whose modern expression was seen in the Ritschlianism of the social gospel movement; (3) the middle position of "Christ above culture" which received its classic formulation in Thomism and attempted to deal with the problem with a "both-and" relationship; (4) the Lutheran dualism of "Christ and culture in paradox" where the allegiance of the Christian was ostensibly divided at different times and in different ways between Christ and Caesar; and finally (5) the Augustinian and Calvinistic viewpoint of "Christ transforming culture" which holds that Christ can, must, and will transform man and society to his ultimate purposes.

That each of these five approaches to the theological problem continues to be a live alternative for the modern Christian there can be no doubt. Our task is to look at the ways in which our churches are now dealing with the problem of culture, particularly as it is highlighted by our high rate of mobility, discerning if we can the theological assumptions implicit in the way we are going about our life and work.

The extent to which mobility has affected the life of our nation as well as the life and work of our churches has been discussed frequently. Modern technological developments, particularly in the areas of transportation and communication as well as our highly productive and prosperous economic situation, have given to an age-old problem of mobility an intensity and magnitude heretofore unknown. When a nation such as ours is confronted by the fact that 30,000,000 of her people move each year, the numerous adjustments and adaptations which must be made in all parts of the social order become apparent. With the physical mobility of peoples come changes which are also sociological and

---

[2]*Christ and Culture*, New York: Harper & Brothers, 1951.

psychological, ideological and spiritual. In the face of these changes the Church is called upon to proclaim its eternal and unchanging Gospel.

In order to make concrete the nature of our theological problem, let us look at one major aspect of the churches' response to the needs of a highly mobile population—the area of church extension, particularly in new communities surounding large central cities. The Congregational-Christian Churches, for example, have helped in the organization and construction of over 100 new churches since 1945. This represents an aggregate capital investment of over $10,000,000, which in turn is but a small part of the $4,000,000,000 which Americans have put into church building construction during the past decade. Judged by economic standards, these have been "boom" years in church extension.

Two recent commentaries on this "boom" in church extension speak directly to our problem. Neither of these writers is a professional churchman, and their comments tend to be more dramatic than typical, more reportorial than scientific. Nevertheless, they bring into bold relief an implicit theological problem and ought to give us pause.

William H. Whyte, Jr., in his recent best-seller entitled *The Organization Man*[3] reports the viewpoint of a Protestant chaplain called by a council of churches to organize a new church in a rapidly growing "package community" outside one of the large metropolitan cities.

He wanted a *useful* church, and to emphasize theological points, he felt, was to emphasize what is not of first importance and at the price of provoking dissension. 'We try not to offend anybody,' he explains.

According to Mr. Whyte this chaplain found that the mobility of residents in this new community had weakened their denominational ties. "In moving from one community to another, many of the transients had gone where there was either no church of their faith or one that to them seemed mediocre, and as a consequence they had got in the habit of 'shopping.' "[4]

And speaking of shopping, Stanley Rowland, Jr., a religious news reporter for the *New York Times*, wrote an article entitled "Suburbia Buys Religion."[5] He suggested that the flocking of

[3]*The Organization Man*, New York: Simon and Schuster, 1956, p. 406. Used by permission.
[4]*Ibid.*, p. 407.
[5]*The Nation*, July 28, 1956. Used by permission.

newer suburbanites to churches and synagogues indicated a drive for cultural and religious identification. He went on to note that

> The main mood of many a suburban church on Sundays is that of a fashionable shopping center. This is cultural identification on a wide, superficial and generally unacknowledged level. On weekdays one shops for food, on Saturdays one shops for recreation and on Sundays one shops for the Holy Ghost.

When cultural values become normative for the "successful" church, the church's very existence is threatened by irrelevance. This is especially true when numbers become the sole criterion of measurement of the church's effectiveness, when a pastor of a "high potential" church gets preoccupied with the exposition of the numerous "facilities" of a new church building or the proclamation of its "friendliness" rather than the exposition of its Scriptures and the proclamation of its good news of man's redemption.

Much of this church extension in new residential communities is done co-operatively and represents a major focus in American interchurch relations. The churches which are established under the aegis of the comity commissions of councils of churches become in every sense "community" churches, ministering to a wide range of Protestants. We point to the diversity of denominational backgrounds represented in the memberships of these churches as the practical fruits of American ecumenicity at the grass-roots level. But this very diversity may suggest a problem often overlooked in ecumenical discourse.

For example, in a recent study of a group of new churches established by one of the leading Protestant denominations it was discovered that less than one fourth of the adult members of these churches were originally members of that denomination and that from thirty to forty per cent of them were received from other denominations by letter of transfer or on reaffirmation of faith. It was further learned that very little formal instruction was given to adults in preparation for church membership. These findings suggested that difficulties faced on the higher levels of the ecumenical conversation with reference to faith and order are apparently more easily transcended on the local level. One reason for this may be that American Protestants are trained more in the school of life and work than in faith and order, and that theological nuances are of little or no concern to the average man in the pew.

201

Or, this may reflect the total absence of any conviction or understanding of one's particular theological tradition or history and the apparent ease with which denominational loyalties can be and are being shifted may not be altogether salutory if we are concerned about the faithfulness of the Church to its purposes.

Furthermore, the principles of comity which underlie the church extension activities of Protestantism tend to be motivated by pragmatic categories such as "competition," "overchurching," "protection," and "economy" rather than theological categories which derive the basis of Christian unity from the Bible and the mission of the Church. Rarely does an interdenominational discussion on comity give more than tacit recognition of the biblical or theological basis for co-operative church planning.

In recent years an interesting distinction has been introduced into the jargon of comity practices. It is the distinction in church extension between "opportunity" and "responsibility." This distinction corresponds to the allocations of suburban sites, on the one hand, and, on the other, the vain pleadings of the councils of churches for denominational support in extending the church in areas of urban redevelopment and renewal in the heart of the city. "Opportunity" refers to allocations in newly developed residential areas; assignments for work in the vicinity of a public housing project or an area of urban renewal are a "responsibility." The distinction merits pondering.

All this would lead us to suggest that the kind of unity we are achieving in American Protestantism may be sociological rather than theological. We see this mainly in terms of a new kind of segregation which is taking place in American life. This is the social and economic segregation which is a consequence of our present pattern of residential mobility. Just as public housing tends to gather together families of low socio-economic status, so private housing, particularly in tract development, tends to sift families according to the cost of their homes. Some denominations prefer to build their new churches in areas of $20,000 homes rather than $10,000 because they assume that they will have a better chance of "succeeding" in such areas. Part of the motivation of people moving to the suburbs and joining our churches may be found in assumptions about social status which are a part of the American social system. Community studies by the Lynds, Warner and his associates, Hollingshead and others have pointed to the role of the churches in ascribing status in American communities. The findings of these sociologists and social anthropologists with reference to the church in American life raise profound questions concerning the purposes of the church and its relationship to culture.

The weight of sociological evidence seems to point to the acculturation of the church in new residential areas occasioned by our present mobility habits. Christ is the Christ *of* Culture, to use Dr. Niebuhr's ideal type.

But studies of new churches also indicate that the fundamental task facing pastors in new communities is to transform a group of people from a diversity of backgrounds into a worshiping congregation of believers, to make of it a gathered community to hear the proclamation of God's Word, to respond to it and to be renewed by it. It is only on the basis of this need for transformation that these new churches can escape annihilation by their surrounding culture.

The obverse side of the suburban church extension picture is the mission we have to the city itself, and particularly to the inner city. The social upheaval occasioned by changing populations, urban renewal and redevelopment is an unparalleled opportunity for the extension of the church. We are acutely aware of the ostensibly negative aspects of this change—the moving away of church families, the deterioration of property, the rising incidence of social disorganization and the influx of new families out of strange cultural backgrounds. Yet it is precisely for this reason that the church in the inner city is confronted by an opportunity to find a new life in Christ.

In the not-too-distant past, the characteristic response of Protestant churches to changes in the inner city was that of fear and flight. Today, whenever a church attempts to remove itself from a changing community, it does so with a sense of unfaithfulness to the Gospel. Yet for those churches which have elected to stay (and of these there are an increasing company), the experience has been one of passing from death into newness of life. This "newness of life" comes to the church only after the fetters of convention and social grace which identified that church in a former era (its "golden age") are abandoned and understanding is achieved of the true meaning and rigor of the Gospel. For many of these churches the sacraments, the liturgy, the nature of the ministry, and indeed the meaning of the Church and the vocation of those gathered to it have become illuminated with spiritual depth and perception heretofore unknown.

In a real sense the vitally concerned, humbly faithful inner-city church has been forced to stand in the midst of its surrounding culture sustained only by its uniqueness as a people of the covenant bearing the radical demands of the Gospel. Here we see no dualism between what is God's and what is Caesar's, for God's demands transcend the injustices perpetrated by the modern Caesar and his petty lieutenants; here Christ does not stand so far above culture that he fails to see the needs of the least of the children but seeks them out in demonstrating the meaning of God's love for his children. All this has required bold and imaginative planning, serious testing of one's spiritual resources and in the end the faithful trusting in God's sufficiency for the tasks at hand.

As an inevitable consequence, this type of ministry has forced the church to rethink its doctrine of the Church and its purpose. It has had to abandon many theological and ecclesiastical niceties for being irrelevant to its true mission and has emerged with a more adequate faith because it has had to restudy the Bible and reappraise the history and traditions of the Church from an entirely new perspective. Often the theological assumptions and liturgical practices, to say nothing of the socio-economic characteristics, of these inner-city churches are unrecognizable alongside the backgrounds and experiences of the denominations to which they belong, but it is this newness of life which comes to the faithful inner-city church that invigorates and gives meaning to the whole body of Christ.

Church extension is but one expression of our mission to America on the move. We have not mentioned our services to migratory laborers, to workers in temporary defense communities, to the millions who are temporarily mobile in search of recreation in our national parks and in tourist centers; nor have we discussed the church in relation to those factors and forces which give rise to mobility in our time—our present trends in industrial organization, national defense, agricultural policy, as well as the emerging problems of our modern society as seen in the context of geriatrics and automation.

Whatever may be said of our basic theological problem, that of the relationship of Christ to culture, it becomes abundantly clear that we are led ultimately to raise the central problem confronting all ecumenical discourse: the nature of the Church and its mission. Whether the context is mobility, or governmental practices and policies, the campus ministry or problems of racial and economic stratification, it is only by returning to the central problem that we begin to comprehend the nature of the unity we seek.

Index

Ainslie, Peter, 24f.
American Baptist Convention, 28
American Lutheran Church, 28
Apostasy, 66, 155
Apostolic ministry, 138ff.
Augsburg Confession, 99f.
Augustana Evangelical Lutheran Church, 28
Aulén, Gustaf, 34
Authority, 90f., 107f., 113, 138f., 143ff.

Baptism, 83f., 86, 108f., 112f., 127, 133ff., 139, 156
Barton, W. E., 24
Boulding, K., 184, 190
Brent, Charles H., 12f., 23
Brown, W. A., 11
Bultmann, Rudolf, 53

Calvin, Jean, 123
Campbell, Alexander, 21
Centralized power, 29f.
Check sheet of Christian belief, 103ff., 111
Chicago-Lambeth Quadrilateral, 22
Chicago, University of, 157
Christian Century, The, 65
Church,
  fellowship in, 134, 163ff., 170, 172f., 188, 198
  invisible, 85, 127ff.
  local, 15f., 20, 75f., 85f., 126ff., 161ff., 170f., 193f.
  as a business enterprise, 183ff.
  as a family, 47f., 52f., 131f., 181ff.
  as a social club, 185ff.
  nature of, 113
  visible, 22, 61, 68, 72, 85, 133f.
Churches of Christ, 123

Concept of church,
  Body of Christ, 55ff., 83f., 106, 121, 161, 164f.
  ekklesia, 43f., 51
  family analogy, 47f., 52f., 131f., 181ff.
  kingdom of God, 44ff., 52
  temple, 49ff., 54f.
Congregational-Christian Churches, 28, 106, 108, 113, 156, 157, 200
Congregations, 163ff., 171
Conn, Howard, 17
Co-operation, 17ff., 23, 28, 64, 67, 87, 109f., 118, 156f.
Councils of churches, 18

Denney, James 87
Denominationalism, 16, 19, 20f., 23f., 29f., 69, 90, 96, 101, 106, 113, 154f., 167, 175, 201
Disciples of Christ, 29, 108, 113, 152, 156, 157
Douglass, H. Paul, 21
Douglass, Truman B., 41, 197

Edinburgh Conference, 1910, 12f., 25, 83
Ellul, J., 48
Episcopacy, 83
Evangelical & Reformed Church, 28, 108, 113
Evangelical Lutheran Church, 28
Evangelical United Brethren, 28, 113
Evanston Report, 76

Faith and Order movement, 12ff., 23f., 27, 29, 83, 92
Federal Council of the Churches of Christ, 11ff., 23

206

Finnish Evangelical Lutheran Church, 28
Forsyth, P. T., 83
Freedom of religion, 20f.

Gardiner, Robert H., 23
Gore, Charles, 87
Greek Orthodoxy, 67
Greenwich plan, 151

Hanson, Stig, 82
Humanism, 67
Huntington, W. R., 22
Hutterian Brethren, 92

Imperatives for unity, 33ff.
Inclusivism, 66f., 71
International missionary council, 12f.
Irenaeus, 137f.

Jehovah's Witnesses, 64
Jenkins, Daniel T., 198

Latourette, Kenneth S., 14
Lausanne Conference, 1927, 13, 23f.
Liberalism, 91f., 123
Life and Work movement, 11ff., 23, 92
Lord's Supper (Eucharist, Holy Communion), 83f., 106, 113, 127, 129f., 133, 139
Lund Conference, 1952, 19
Luther, Martin, 123
Lutheran Church–Missouri Synod, 61, 99ff., 108, 112f., 123, 157

Mackay, John A., 88
Mar Thoma Church, 42
Mennonite, 89, 199
Methodist Church, 28f., 85, 109, 112f., 156
Ministry, types of,
education, 172f.
evangelization, 172f.
fellowship, 172f.
worship, 172f.
Minneapolis study committee, 109
Missionary movement, 12, 118
Mission Covenant Church, 106, 108, 113f.
Moody, Dwight L., 92

Motives for unity,
Christian, 39ff.
non-Christian, 37ff.
others, 40ff.
Mott, John R., 12

National Council of Churches, 23
Newbigin, J. E. L., 17, 84
Newman, John Henry, 88
Niebuhr, H. Richard, 24, 171, 192, 199, 203
Niebuhr, Reinhold, 170

Oberlin Conference, 1957, 26f., 157, 197
One church, 21, 23, 25ff., 128, 148, 150f.
Oppenheimer, J. Robert, 190
Oxnam, G. Bromley, 64

Person of Christ, 83, 106, 113f.
Pope, Lisyon, 179
Presbyterian Church in U.S.A., 28, 85, 109, 112f., 157
Protestant Episcopal Church, 28f., 108, 113, 121, 152, 156, 157, 166f.
Prounion, 62f.

Quakers (Society of Friends), 92, 147, 157

Reformation, The, 91, 99, 156, 190
Reformed Church in America, 28, 157
Roman Catholicism, 37, 42, 64, 67, 72, 90, 121ff., 147, 170
Rowland, S., 200

Salvation, 108, 113f.
Schaff, Philip, 22
Schmucker, S. S., 22
Separatism, 62f., 64, 66f.
Social action, 12, 27, 30, 197f.
Söderblom, Nathan, 12, 23
Southern Baptist Convention, 61, 84ff., 106, 108, 113, 122, 152, 156, 157
Stockholm Conference, 1925, 12, 18

Temple, William, 13, 153
Theological interest, 25f., 30, 110ff., 201

Thils, Gustav, 75
Troeltsch, Ernst, 191

Una Sancta, 75f., 80, 83, 146
Union movements, 28f.
Unitarians, 64, 67, 157
United Church of Canada, 28
United Church of Christ, 28
United Evangelical Lutheran
Church, 28
United Lutheran Church of
America, 28f., 154
United Presbyterian Church of
North America, 28

Universal Christian Conference, *see*
Stockholm

View of the Bible, 113f.
Visser 't Hooft, W. A., 73, 98, 119

Weigel, Gustave, 38, 42
Whyte, W. H., 200
World Council of Churches, 13, 42,
64, 75ff., 87f., 98, 118, 125
World Missionary Conference, *see*
Edinburgh
World-wide church, 15f.

Yoder, Don H., 21f.